SCHOOL DAZE

SCHOOL DAZE

Helping Parents Cope With The
Bewildering World of Public Schools

BILL SANDERS

Fleming H. Revell Company
Tarrytown, New York

Library of Congress Cataloging-in-Publication Data

Sanders, Bill, date
    School daze / Bill Sanders.
        p.   cm.
    Includes bibliographical references (p.   ).
    ISBN 0-8007-1666-3
    1. Education—United States—Parent participation.   2. Teenagers—United States—Attitudes.   3. Home and school—United States.
    I. Title.
    LB1048.5.S26   1992
    370.19'31'0973—dc20   91-37903
                                                        CIP

Copyright © 1992 by Bill Sanders
Published by the Fleming H. Revell Company
Tarrytown, New York 10591

Printed in the United States of America

This is one of the most important pages in this book. Without these people, I would never be able to challenge public-school students with the sound Christian principles that make America great.

TO the hundreds of principals, superintendents, activity coordinators, and countless others who have entrusted me with their students, teachers, and parents for an entire day, I'd like to express my deep appreciation. If you didn't believe that I could truly make a big difference in people's lives, I never would have had a chance to creatively teach right from wrong.

TO the hundreds of teachers, parents, grandparents, students, businessmen and businesswomen who come up to me after my evening community session and say, "Thanks for creatively and tactfully bringing God to our school today. You've modeled for all of us that we needn't ever be ashamed of our faith and what made us strong in the first place."

TO the students—thousands of you have allowed me to cry with you, laugh with you, answer your letters, hurt with you, instill hope in you, and shared my best friend, Jesus Christ, with you. Thousands more of you have stood at the end of the assemblies, indicating to the world that you choose not to drink alcohol or use drugs again. Hundreds have told me you were planning to give up your virginity that weekend, but because of my talk you are saving yourselves for marriage only! I give up my family over a hundred days a year for all of you. You are worth it! You have what it takes to make the right decisions, and I feel confident in handing over a deeply troubled world to you—our future parents and leaders.

TO Josh McDowell, Art Linkletter, Bill Hybels, Norm Wright, Tony Campolo, Scott Taveau, and Zig Ziglar for your excitement about this book, but mostly for your endorsing me personally. I promise I won't let our young people down.

TO my secretary, office manager, my brains, my voice to schools before and after each and every speaking engagement, Kathy Reisner. Thank you! Thank you for your belief in me and your unending love for Jesus and all of His hurting kids. You answer their letters, visit them in jail, weekly encourage them in the juvenile home, a probation officer to some, big sister to countless others, counselor to them each summer; you pray for them each night and hurt for so many of them daily. May God always bless you for helping "the least of these."

TO my loving, laughing and extrasupportive family. Holly, you are always there for me when I get home—smiling and hugging and telling me you are proud of me. You raise our children while I'm gone and never make me feel guilty for the time I'm away from home. You encourage me to follow my convictions and to speak out the truths the Lord has laid on my heart. My enthusiastic children not only give me tons of special material, but tons of XOXOXOXOXO as well!

Finally, but most importantly, thank You, Jesus. You have given me a message of hope and love to share in a place I'm not supposed to share it, our public schools. You have placed me there for a reason. You have given me the passion, the humor, and the boldness to say that I'm not speaking to gain friends, but to help people avoid scars and pains. You show me daily that you're still in the miracle business. As long as I have a voice and the strength to physically stand up to the thirteen-hour days, I'll be Your beacon in helping them miss the jagged rocks waiting to destroy them. My goal is to "give 'em heaven!"

CONTENTS

Part III: What Are Our Children Taught?

PREFACE
WHAT THIS BOOK IS—
AND IS NOT

Rest assured that I do not hate our school systems. It is not my purpose to start a witch-hunt or focus on all the awful things that appear in our press. I spend over a hundred days a year in our schools. When I talk, I try to reach, teach, and give hope to our future—America's young people. But that does not mean I turn a blind eye to everything negative. I know the hurts of the teens who are left out at school and home, who seem to have no one to turn to.

Because I know of the hurt teens experience, I would like to challenge parents and members of the school system to realize that our children need help. They need our prayers and every ounce of energy we can give them, to give them strength through a difficult time.

Today pressures on teens have reached huge dimensions. They face the deadly impact of AIDS, crack cocaine, marijuana laced with deadly poisons, and ten times the number of sexually transmitted diseases that existed three decades ago. Because they also have more spending money than any generation in mankind's history, the temptations are great.

I'd like to see parents, school personnel, and community work together as one large team to reach our kids. As I've written, I've tried not to patronize parents or teachers. Instead I want to take an honest look at issues and concerns. I want parents to become aware that some teachers have the dedication to give their lives during the school day; in the middle of July; and at 12:30 A.M., when a troubled student calls to talk things over.

Sure, some teachers should make a career change—but this only applies to a small percentage of them. Others simply need help to become real life touchers, not just fact-giving machines.

It would be unfair to both parents and teachers if I did not deal with some of the hot potatoes of education, so I have included them in Part III. Parents and teachers need to be aware of some of the threats to family life and the strong moral base that will make our schools more effective. As I write about these, I am not hunting out witches. I do not mean to point the finger or make parents overly nervous. But I speak to teens every year without pulling punches. During many of my assemblies I wear a T-shirt that reads: *Right is right—Wrong is wrong . . . Have the courage to sing the right song.* When I tell them the truth at every opportunity, how can I do any less to parents and teachers? I need to have the courage of my convictions. And those who are most concerned with the schools need to know what's going on.

So the focus of this book is not to attack, but build up. I want to give you an inside view of your child's feelings. Based on my experience with teens and the survey of 7,500 of them that appears in Appendix I, I hope I can help you understand why you have to learn a different language to speak to your children. How else can a parent know why earrings are in and shoelaces are out, or why teens have an unquenchable thirst for music, videos, and media filled with horror, degrading themes, drugs, hopelessness, and rebellion?

The hurting teen who clams up and won't talk to Mom and Dad desperately needs them. He may not want his parents near him and won't be seen with them, especially in public, but he still needs their support. When he seems happy and things are going good and he's talking freely, he's easiest to reach, but that's when he needs his parents the least.

Parenting teens is a strange mission field. Sometimes they can be sarcastic and belligerent, but at other times they become loving, kind, and gentle. When they need us, they're often too cool or proud to ask.

By sharing with you the troubles teens have expressed to me, I hope to help you understand your son or daughter better than you have in a long time. As you comprehend the pressures your teen faces, I hope that you will develop a plan that will make you a valuable resource in his or her life. You can have the greatest impact on your child, and I want to help you do that—through a loving hug before and after a date and as an advisor your teen turns to with the problems that face her, even though she seems to be growing up "too fast."

I want you to be successful with your mission, and I pray these tools will help.

INTRODUCTION

A child is a person who is going to carry on what you have started. . . . Sit where you are sitting, and when you are gone, attend to those things you think are important. . . . The child will assume control of your cities, states, and nations. . . . Move in and take over your churches, schools, universities, and corporations. . . . The fate of humanity is in the hands of children. . . .

Abraham Lincoln

Children are one of our nation's greatest resources. They are our most important one, in fact, because someday they will take over our places in the world—and what they think about the world, themselves, and others will change it forever.

Today parents often wonder what's become of the world, and when they look into the future, they worry about their children. How can they help them become successful? Will their young people have what it takes to live well? How can parents protect them from the negative influences around them?

Often we point the finger at education. "The schools should do a better job. Just look at what my daughter brought home from school yesterday!" frustrated parents may cry. Meanwhile teachers exclaim, "If parents would only do their job, we wouldn't have to take on another task!"

What is happening in our schools? How have things failed to work, and how can we change failure to success?

The Start of Education

Most people think of education as beginning when a child goes to a preschool, nursery school, or otherwise begins formal schooling. But by having that understanding, they miss out on the learning that takes place in those important first few years of life. The child who will one day run this nation or its most prestigious church, school, or business began to learn at home. Education begins there, because parents have a strong influence on their children.

Ideally Mom and Dad can teach their son that in their house he can safely risk, learn, try, fail, rebound, and try again. They can show their daughter what it means to be truthful, faithful, and caring. Home becomes a place of challenge and comfort.

Mixed Messages?

Even when they aren't consciously teaching, parents implant their ideas in their children. Each day, youngsters learn from how their mom and dad react to situations, what they say, and what they believe—we call this modeling. The Bible gives us a look at effective modeling when it commands:

> Love the Lord your God with all your heart and with all your soul and with all your strength. These commandments that I give you today are to be upon your hearts. Impress them on your children. Talk about them when you sit at home and when you walk along the road, when you lie down and when you get up. Tie them as symbols on your hands and bind them on your foreheads. Write them on the doorframes of your houses and on your gates.
>
> Deuteronomy 6:5–9

That does not describe a once-a-week, parent-to-child sermon, but a daily way of life that teaches youngsters right from wrong.

The modeling a child receives in the home will have a powerful impact on his or her future, but it is not the only influence. Many parents want their children to have good examples in the home. They seek to instill good values there, only to find that the world around them has a different idea. When they look at the schools, they wonder how their children will fare in this large, sometimes dangerous world.

The world wants to plant its agendas on each child's mind and heart. In the nineties, anything goes. So often families see the world going in a different direction—one totally opposite to their own. Though they disapprove of the world's message, parents may feel at a loss, not knowing how to respond to it or help their teens avoid the confusion it creates.

To understand what is happening in a child's life, parents need to become aware of what the school and community are saying to children; they need to become aware of the influence a boy or girl's friends have upon that child. Mom and Dad can then begin to effectively counterbalance the influences that will not glorify God. Once they have the evidence, they can show teens the harm of drugs, premarital sex, and other immoral behavior.

Schools and Communities

The problems parents see in schools are not isolated—really they exist in the community at large. If a town has a morality problem, it will show up in the schools. When adults use drugs and alcohol, engage in premarital sex, use profanity, and take part in stealing, lying, and cheating, so will the children. For many years I have said there is no such thing as a drug problem in our schools—but there is one in our communities. Remember, as parents, "we cannot not model"! We are modeling all the time, whether or not we like it.

Whatever happens in our towns and cities appears in our schools, because the young people simply bring beliefs and ways of life they have already learned into school with them. What they have picked up at home and in the streets becomes part of themselves.

The greatest place of teaching is the home. When a child sees integrity or indifference, love or hate, solutions for problems worked out in the home or an evasion of responsibility, he or she automatically reproduces that. Every day of their lives parents model behavior. Some kids have good homes—and some have not-so-good ones—but whichever they have, they use that as they learn to speak, walk, and feel good or bad about themselves.

Parents worry about the things that go on in their schools—and they should be concerned about their youngsters' environment. They need to know which teachers care for their children, teaching them the difference between right and wrong, helping them develop stable life-styles, and so on. They need to become aware of what the school teaches. The school system that has a very different agenda from its community—that teaches harmful ideas or subjects beyond its calling—should be held accountable by the parents and community. When parents discover these things, they need to take loving action.

When parents have failed to care for their children, school administrators may have to intervene in family life, but that is not generally part of a school's role. When schools take on parental roles, they have gone too far—and parents should object.

To avoid negative attitudes about parents in education, Mom and Dad can make good family life a priority. Parents can legitimately request that the school stick to education, once family life is well cared for in the home.

For those who struggle with the issues of education and homelife, I'd like to share a Scripture of hope: "Train a child in the way he should go, and when he is old he will not turn from it" (Proverbs 22:6). I do not believe now is the time to give up—for the good of our teens and our communities, we need to seek to understand and take part in our schools, towns, and cities.

SCHOOL DAZE

Part I
A SCHOOL IS MORE THAN JUST A BUILDING

Before we look at the situation our schools are in, we need to understand our own homes and communities. What do we find there, and what needs to change? Once we know how home, community, and school can work together for a better environment, parents, leaders, and teachers can cooperate to create the best public school possible.

1
MEETING A CHILD'S MOST BASIC NEEDS

When I visit a school system, I'm only there for a short time. While I'm with the students, I talk to them about what it's like to be less than perfectly secure. I share my own pain at being the tall, gangly kid who towered above his classmates. I let them know it's okay not to be the class athlete or the prettiest girl. Maybe that's why they feel they can share their lives with me.

When I leave, I make sure the students have my address, and each year I receive thousands of letters, especially from hurting teens. In fact it's gotten to the point where I can almost predict how many letters I will get from a school and what topics they will cover. If I see them squirm when I talk about certain drug issues, or if they become loud when I speak about peer pressure, or if they hoot and holler and glamorize drinking when I tell them about its dangers, I know I've hit a hot spot.

But why do these teens listen to my talks, answer my questionnaire on their problems, talk to me after my speech, write to me at home, and seem to seek the answers I've provided in my book *Life, Sex, and Everything in Between?* I think it's because they can tell that I have time for them, that I care about them, and I want to help them. They know I know what it is to be less than perfect and that I'll accept them when they aren't, too. They also know I won't be around long enough to take them to task for anything.

I can't be there every day for your teen, but *you* can. Believe it or not, your child needs you. You can offer your teen:

> Communication
> A long-term viewpoint
> Acceptance
> Input and response

They are critical to any young person's well-being.

A Teen Needs Communication

It saddens me to think that so many children feel they cannot speak to Mom or Dad. When a youngster thinks her parents are too busy, she won't want to interrupt—even if Mom or Dad would love to know what's on her mind. If Dad is never there, or if he makes it clear that, when he is around home, he'd prefer to be perfecting his golf game, working on a second master's degree, or going for the big raise and promotion at the office, his son will feel like an intrusion.

Some of the young people I hear from are abused physically—but many more have been abused by the neglect of parents who seem too busy to spend time with their children. Some teens who have suffered such a lack of attention have shared truly horrifying stories. I see letters that show me that they need to know what love is—and what it isn't; that demonstrate that they will search in all the wrong places for happiness—unless Mom and Dad show them the right places; that prove that young people need to learn communication skills and the art of forgiving.

Chances are that, deep down, your child wants to communicate. Perhaps opening the door to it will be difficult, but it will be worth your efforts. Take the time to discover how your son feels or what your daughter is doing. It may take patience, time, and intense caring, but it can happen! You can spend time now, preparing your child for the world, or later on, repairing his or her mistakes. It's much easier to take the time now.

A Teen Needs a Long-term Viewpoint

Recently, I asked a group of students: "How many of you know that this biblical lesson is a good way to keep your relationships right? Fill in the blank." Then I said, "Never let the sun go down on your _____ "

Believe it or not, someone yelled out, "Head!"

We all had a good laugh, but it made me realize that many youngsters have never heard that you can keep your relationship—with a spouse, parent, or child—strong if you don't let the sun go down on your anger. They have never learned to work problems through by the day's end. This works in my home, but I must admit that last month my wife and I were up two weeks straight! (Just joking!)

"This, too, shall pass," my grandmother taught me, and I'm glad she did. Kids need to learn that they can have a long-term view of problems. Today's zit or heartache need not be unhappiness tomorrow. That zit will go away. That heartache can be dealt with now instead of being left to fester.

Parents can help their children by fostering an attitude that focuses on long-term goals. When Mom and Dad combine this with consistent hope and encouragement, they help teens know that even if they fail today, they can retain their parents' love, understanding, and friendship. However, your children won't learn this unless you tell them over and over again.

A Teen Needs Acceptance

Kids desperately need to be liked and accepted. But even if you say something loving on Monday, your daughter may not still believe it on Tuesday. *Every day*, pass on the message, "You are special. God made you in His image."

As you accept your child, correct one common mistake in education. Let him know he not only has your acceptance—he can have God's, too. Let him know that evolution is a bunch of garbage, that he has a Creator who cares for him and knows what he is going through. Encourage him to know God.

Often schools specifically request that I talk about self-esteem and self-worth. Their young people are making the wrong choices—having sex before marriage, using drugs, going to booze parties, and so on. The administrators come to me to make their students feel good about themselves. They think that once I've given the students a talk, they'll feel so pumped up, they'll change their behavior.

"How can I help their esteem," I ask, "when you tell them they were made from slime and life has no purpose? Unless I tell them that their fingerprints are different because God made them that way and that each has special talents, they won't have anything to base good self-esteem on. As long as people compare themselves with others, they will never have true success. I have to tell them that there is something greater in life, and God is still in control."

No school has become upset with me for telling young people that God made them and they have awesome potential inside them—that each one of them was no mistake. I appreciate the schools' attitude in that.

A Teen Needs Input and Response

To have the kind of hope that lasts, children need to have input into their parents' lives. They need time to ask questions, to share their fears, and to be part of what goes on in the family.

Your children desperately want to help you decide which car to buy or plan your next vacation. They want you to really listen when they share an idea for a really creative vacation—even though it might not be what you had in mind.

The child who knows he has been really listened to will feel needed and wanted and will know he has contributed to the family. Without that, he will feel aimless and hopeless. Instead of going to Mom and Dad for love and support, he will find it in the alleys, in the backseat of a car, or in a gang that makes him feel wanted.

But that doesn't mean Mom or Dad should be a pushover. The letters I receive tell me that young people want answers. They don't want a wishy-washy adult to tell them, "Do your own thing, whatever feels good." They need to know what is right and wrong. When they forget, Mom or Dad needs to repeat the message, "Some things will not be tolerated—and this is one of those things." Just as the law will not allow people to act certain ways, parents need to take firm stands on their children's actions. They must give a response that is in the teens' best interests. Teens will never respect society's laws if they never see laws at home. Remember, you can *prepare* or *repair* your teens!

Most homes could use at least some improvement in these areas. Start to make them a part of your homelife today. Then you can begin to plan to reach out to the community around you to share these truths. You can't expect to improve your community until you have your own house in order; but once you've gotten good communication with your teens, imagine how you could expand that to her friends, their families, and the school system.

Action Plan for Parents

Take some time to consider ways in which you can meet your child's needs. Read the following suggestions and then come up with a few of your own.

1. How is communication between you and your child? Take an inventory. Do you have a disagreement that needs talking out? Do you need to apologize to your son or daughter? Is there an issue you've been afraid to confront with your child? Once you've completed your inventory, think of some creative ways you can begin to deal with the problems.

2. Write a letter to your child, expressing your love. Remember some of the good times you've had together and give some encouragement concerning the rough spots your child may face. Without putting pressure on your teen, perhaps you will want to share some goals you'd like to accomplish in the future.

Remember, your goal is to establish loving communication. Do not attack your child or unnecessarily create a negative situation.

3. If there are deep troubles in your family life, and you cannot communicate, perhaps you will need to consider counseling. Discover the resources in your community by contacting your pastor, a school guidance counselor, or local agencies. Before you become involved in counseling, though, discover what the attitudes of the counselor are. You will want the most positive support available for your family, and you will want someone who believes in God and the time-tested and proven principles found in His Book.

2

YOU CAN'T TAKE THE SCHOOL OUT OF THE COMMUNITY

When I walk into a school, I can often tell what the surrounding community is like.

Often I speak in towns with a strong, supportive family base. I can tell what the community is like by the way the kids listen, the respect they give me, and their overall politeness. What they learned at home becomes part of their school days.

In other towns I have a continual uphill battle to keep the teens' attention during the assembly.

You can't place the community in one box and its students in another. Because teens live in the real world, so do the schools. Often we try to ignore that fact.

The communities that hold our schools are more diverse than many of us imagine. Here are a few stories from my own experiences.

One evening a counselor picked me up at the airport. On the way to the school, he warned me not to mention anything "controversial"—especially if it had to do with right and wrong or God and religion. When I asked why, he shared that the school was under so much pressure from the "radical right"—as some people call Bible-believing Christians—

and the atheists that the school system had turned into a battleground. Some Christians had become so afraid that they would not even publicly bow their heads and say a silent prayer before a meal.

As I spoke with the students in this community, I noticed some interesting things. During the elementary session, I asked the kids who made our fingerprints different. Not a child raised his or her hand. About three hundred grammar-school children sat there with their mouths open, but no one answered. Never before in the thirteen years I've spoken in schools had this happened.

"Come on," I prompted them. "You know who made our thumbprints different. Who is it?"

Finally one brave sixth grader in the back of the room raised his hand and quietly said, "The man upstairs."

That evening, when I spoke with parents, I shared with them the fact that community pressures had reduced the Creator of the universe to "the man upstairs" in the minds of their children. I thought that it was a sad day for that town when their young people became too afraid to share the truth that God made their fingerprints just for them.

The fear that I saw in those children did not come about all on its own. The pressure of the community had worked its way into the school.

In a midwest town on the border of two states, all day long I heard about "the Party." Several hundred teens had attended it, and it had lasted two days. Parents had left two homes conveniently empty, so their kids could stay home and party, with many kegs of beer for all comers. Needless to say, it was a wild occasion. The entire town, which had a population of about 10,000, talked about it.

When I spoke in the evening, I asked the nearly nine-hundred adults and teens who attended, "How many of you know it is illegal for teens to drink?" Everyone raised a hand.

"How many of you know that teens could have been raped during the party—inside or outside of the houses—especially since it wasn't chaperoned, and teens were free to come and go?" Again all hands were raised. This group also knew that the teens who attended the party could have gotten into deep trouble and that lives could have been lost because of the activities that went on at the party.

Then the big question: "How many of you called the cops and told them to raid the party, because the young people needed a lifelong lesson that illegal is illegal? Did you tell them that putting teens in jail would be worth it if it saved lives?"

Not a hand was raised.

I turned to a father in the front row. "I don't mean to pick on you, sir," I told him. "But I want to use you as an example.

"What would you have done if you had looked out of your window and noticed a teenager stealing a stereo out of your neighbor's car?"

Without hesitation, he boldly responded, "I would have called the cops."

"Listen, folks. By your actions this weekend you just told me that a two-hundred-dollar stereo is more important than seventy to eighty percent of the young people in this town.

"If we are not committed enough to model right and wrong in front of our kids, and if we are not committed enough to set an example and show them that some things will not be tolerated, our young people will stay confused forever. They will never learn firsthand—from us, their leaders, parents, neighbors, and teachers—how to live according to the law."

A few years ago, some area churches brought me into a school. I don't really like a situation like that, because the school that doesn't have an investment in my presentation is likely to see it as being of little importance. This was a perfect case in point.

Because the churches had footed the bill, the principal didn't attend.

A student got up to introduce me. The kids were so loud that they couldn't hear a word he said. When he had yelled for about ten minutes, they still hadn't settled down.

Still no sign of the principal.

After about twenty-five minutes, the nearly 1,500 students quieted down. My eighty-minute presentation was reduced to about forty minutes, so I could only hit some of the key topics. I briefly touched on self-esteem, peer pressure, alcohol, drugs, and sex.

When I got to the premarital sex part, the crowd seemed stunned. As I told it like it is, I noticed girls throughout the auditorium beginning to weep.

I could sense they had been sexually abused in some way or that they had given up their virginity and regretted it deeply.

I concluded with the words: "If you have lost your virginity by force, please remember that you are still a virgin in God's eyes. And if you've given it up by choice, I challenge you to become a 'second-chance virgin.' Save yourself from this moment until you get married. I will leave my name and address on this pamphlet. If you write to me, I will answer you personally.

"Thank you, I appreciate your time. God bless you! Have a super day." The assembly was over, and the students gave me a wonderful round of applause.

For the next three hours several hundred kids stayed behind, lined up to talk to me. Many of them cried and told me they needed counseling and wanted help.

Several told me that in the large university nearby, they had been admitted to parties, free of charge, as long as they got drunk and were sexually active with the students there.

Every seventh or eighth person informed me that because I had twice said *God* in the assembly, his or her parents would be informed. I might be sued.

After a while, I felt as if the students had been rehearsed. Either they were totally touched by my talk, or they were full of anger because I had stepped on their rights by briefly mentioning God.

As I was counseling students, one girl ran up, grabbed my arm, and cried out, "You must come over here. My friend was going to commit suicide, but you saved her life."

I turned to the other student, who was sobbing and shaking. She handed me a bottle of pills she had planned on taking later. That morning she had wanted to take her own life. But my talk had made sense to her and had given her a new hope. She wanted help.

Though I'd been talking to teens for forty-five minutes after my presentation, no counselor, teacher, or administrator had checked to see why so many kids had not come back to class. I didn't have a counselor to help her. Instead, I'd begun grabbing kids who seemed to have it together and pairing them with the hurting ones. At least that way the teens who needed help had someone to listen to them.

This girl needed a trained counselor, so I sent another student to find one. When that counselor came, I handed over the pills. Later I found out that the teen had been taken to a rehabilitation center.

The high school in that liberal university town was simply typical of the community. The philosophy of life in the town filtered down to the students I talked to, but they were hurting because they'd followed it.

No one sued me for mentioning God, but a parent did write to the local newspaper, objecting to my talk. The newspaper, which took my words totally out of context, had headlines like "Bill Sanders Was Preaching to Students" and "Bill Sanders Called Our Kids Sinners if They Had Sex, Praise the Lord."

I have never said such things in public—especially in the public schools. Though I tell kids they need creative refusal skills and show them how to avoid premarital sex, drugs, alcohol, cigarettes, profanity, stealing, and so on, I do not step on my privilege. I do not come in to give a religious talk or say anything that will step on the school's authority.

No one asked my opinion of the articles or tried to verify that I *had* said such things. The local newspaper printed the story, and Associated Press picked up on it. As a result—since they *did* spell my name right—I've booked so many speeches that the article became the best free promotion I've ever had!

That school was not the only place where teens cried out for help. In another the administrators asked me to be available to talk to students after the program. During the assembly I announced that I would be available, but that each student who wanted to talk to me must write out his or her hurt on one page, in case I didn't get to all of them. I wanted to write to the students I couldn't speak to.

When I and a couple of counselors went to the room the school had provided, over a hundred teens appeared, papers filled.

Because I didn't have much time, I asked if someone would like to share. Some girls got up and began to talk about their pain and the help my speech had given them. But this wasn't the appropriate place to share many deep hurts, so I quickly suggested that we end the discussion, and we collected the papers.

As I read through them with the counselor, I exclaimed, "This is unbelievable! You have here the hundred most hurting kids in the school, with their problems identified, and they want help. What can we do to get it for them?" I knew this was not my area of expertise, and the next day I would be gone. I wanted to make sure these teens were not ignored.

A few days later, I called the school, to ask what I could do, besides writing to students and sending them my books and tapes.

The school told me they had done away with the letters; they had not called on any of the local social agencies. None of the staff counselors had met with these students.

When I expressed my outrage, they complained, "You stirred up something, and then you abandoned us. You left us here, holding the bag, with one hundred emotionally messed-up kids wanting to talk about their problems. We are not experts in that area."

"Maybe so," I countered, "but let's get them the help they need. Call in area counselors and experts. You have identified the students who are crying out for help. They have told you how they are hurting. This is not right."

I could do no more, though I hurt for those students. It seemed as if the school totally denied that their children hurt and needed help.

I'm not saying that your community is necessarily like any of these. Most of the schools I speak in are very positive. About 98 percent of the presentations I make receive rave reviews from parents, teachers, community members, and teens. But it's easier to see that the community influences the schools when you see a problem.

Every one of us needs to feel concern about our schools, because they reflect the image of our communities. The school system becomes a mirror that reflects our own ideals.

Parents hold a particularly important role in the schools. If they never visit, they can have no impact on them. When teachers and administrators see no parental influence, they begin to think that they must take on the parenting role, too.

Mom and Dad, let's try to understand the communities we live in and work hand in hand with the school to reach, teach, and touch the lives of our children.

Action Plan for Parents

1. Take a look at your community. What are its basic values? To discover this, you may want to read through a local newspaper or outline some of the most recent issues that have become a part of the community

life. What values can you see in the school system? How have they gotten there?

2. What role are you playing in the community? List the groups you take part in within your town or city. What role do you take in nearby communities; how can this impact your own?

3. Can you see some ways in which you need to become part of community life? Have you encouraged your children to reach out to others in the community? Develop an action plan that will help your family touch the people around you.

4. What do you know about your local paper? Is it liberal and seemingly against family issues, or is it supportive of family and godly ideals? Write your thoughts to the editors—provide an opposing viewpoint or encouragement, depending on the paper's outlook. Let your views be known.

3
TAKE A LOOK AT YOUR SCHOOL ENVIRONMENT

I know you've heard all the horror stories about how our schools are failing our children. In the newspapers and other media, we continually hear about the troubles that afflict our schools. But how often do you hear about the loving, caring, dedicated people who teach our children? How often does someone commend these overworked, underpaid people who receive little appreciation or prestige?

Public perception says, "Those who can, do; and those who can't, teach." An attitude like that discourages teachers and doesn't place much emphasis upon the important job they have. After all, if a teacher has my child in his classroom for over a thousand hours each year, he will do much more than teach math or help her discover the capital of Michigan or Alabama. That teacher imparts to my child how he feels about himself and how adults respond to life itself.

When teachers are degraded, how can one feel he can make a difference in someone's life, give a sturdy handshake, and impart a sense of confidence to my child? As long as teachers feel like second-class citizens, they can't do a very good job.

Parents, we need to encourage teachers, build them up, and get in touch with them when they do little things that please us. When was the last time you made a phone call or wrote a note thanking a teacher?

Have you ever worked for someone who just waited to see you goof up before he gave you attention? You could count on having only unpleasant experiences with him, and soon you resented it. Well, teachers feel the same way when parents wait for them to go wrong before they open their mouths. But it doesn't have to be that way. Communication can exist on both sides of the parent-teacher relationship.

When I speak to teachers, I challenge them to get ahold of parents at the beginning of the year and discover what areas they can help each child in, apart from the subject matter. An extra shy student could benefit from taking part in public speaking, asking questions, or being a special helper. Or a parent may be able to share effective ways to deal with a rambunctious child. Without talking to parents, a teacher will never know about growth areas in a child's life.

Parents may also need to communicate about areas they don't want to become part of their child's life. After all, when a teacher instills thoughts and ideals that do not support the family structure, parents have a right to object. I have taught my children to say "never" to drugs, and I don't want a teacher telling my child, "You can decide for yourself. If it feels good. . . ." When I teach my child to say no to sex, I don't appreciate a teacher claiming, "Do what you feel is good now. If you'd enjoy it, what can be wrong?" That's the sort of thing I want my child excluded from.

By communicating with a teacher from the very first, I can earn the right to share the things that I do not want my child to learn. When I only object, I will tear a teacher down, but when I can encourage a teacher, because I know the good things she has done, I will more clearly be able to point out flaws in a specific program.

A lot more goes on in our schools than reading, writing, and arithmetic. Even though many teachers feel tired, they go the extra mile. Last week I heard about a math teacher who has never before counseled or worked with hurting kids. But he befriended a hurting student who felt ready to drop out of school. As a child, she had been abused, and for years she had hidden her pain. As this teacher met with her for three or four months, she has become excited about her future. She has worked through much of the hurt that she felt she could never share with her parents.

There are so many good teachers out there. Give them the support they need. Shake their hands, tell them you appreciate them, and spend time with them. Our teachers need our support, and we need theirs!

Supporting Your School

On a typical work day, I spend time inside one junior high and two high schools, holding three different assemblies, each an hour and a half long. In the afternoon, I may do a forty-five-minute presentation for teachers. Then in the evening I spend an hour and a half talking to parents and the community at large.

When I speak, I give a strong message that differentiates right from wrong. My reputation for knowing about the issues teens face and for being a Christian—without any apologies for that—has often preceded me. But the schools I speak in also know that when I mention my faith it will be tactfully and professionally. I'm not a preacher.

When I speak to parents and students, I tell them that I think we compromise when we teach students we're against drunk driving—but don't address the fact that drinking is against the law for our kids. I tell students that responsible use is a bunch of malarkey. "Just as you cannot 'responsibly' murder someone, a teen can't responsibly drink," I explain. "They're both against the law."

I tell teens not to have "safe sex"—don't have sex at all! "Would it be logical for us to say that if you can't find something 'right' about something, there is something wrong with it?" I suggest. (Most people hate the *W* word—*wrong*. They think you shouldn't use it anywhere except at church.) For many years now I've added this question: "What is right about a teenager having multiple sex experiences, with multiple sex partners, prior to marriage?" No one has ever given me a strong answer to that question.

I appreciate that schools let me share these messages. Never yet has one gotten angry with me for saying that right is right and wrong is wrong, and we cannot decide when and where to use situational ethics. Schools also don't get angry when I share that when it comes to peer pressure and saying never to drugs teens can make the decisions themselves.

Students have written me and shared that they were considering suicide and decided not to or they say they are depressed and are considering suicide, or they explain that they are being seriously abused. I always call to let the school know that child needs help, and the people there react with the utmost concern for the child. I appreciate that. And the lives of many students depend upon it.

So many of the people who staff our schools want the best for our young people. They deserve our support. If you do find out that your school has a poor agenda, you may still be able to tactfully and prayerfully seek change. But to know that and do that, you need to become aware of the lessons your teachers are putting before your children, the ideas they focus on, and the people who influence them.

When you carefully and lovingly share the concerns of your heart, keeping the best interests of the students, community, and teachers in mind, you will be able to successfully communicate your vision for the school and family. Take steps to develop that vision!

Our public school system is not hopeless. But it needs the input of concerned parents and teachers who are willing to take the time to make schools the best they can be.

Action Plan for Parents

1. Have you had contact with your child's teachers? If not, think up an action plan for good communication. Can you call, write, or meet with your child's teacher or guidance counselor?

2. If your child has more than one teacher, which ones are favorites? Which are not so special? Why? Talk to your child for input in these areas.

3. Does your child have subjects in which he or she is especially strong? Does this influence his or her opinion of the people who teach those courses? If your child has some "problem areas," work together with the teacher, child, and school officials to create a solution. Perhaps tutoring or some special assignments can help.

4. How can you express your thanks to a teacher who has helped your child? Think of some good ways to express appreciation. Has a teacher gone the extra mile or just been faithful on a day-by-day basis? Be sure you tell that person what it has meant to you and your teen.

5. What vision do you have for your schools? Is it realistic? Does it take into account the resources of the teachers, students, and community? Have you shared that vision with a teacher or school leader? How can it become part of your school system?

Part II
A TEEN'S-EYE VIEW
OF LIFE

What's school like today? Many parents find it bewildering, so I asked for some help—from their own teens. I gave 7,500 students an anonymous survey that asked about their environment at home and in school. We covered issues such as self-esteem, family life, and problem solving, in addition to the drug, sex, and education issues. As far as possible, I believe most teens gave me from-the-heart answers. Many seemed to show a compelling honesty.

Though I asked over thirty questions (for the complete survey and exhaustive answers, *see* Appendix I), here all are covered topically, under seven major questions teens could ask themselves.

May the answers provide parents with insight and information that will help them understand their teens.

4

HOW DO I FEEL ABOUT MYSELF?

Parents want their children to have healthy self-esteem. However, as Ken Abraham says, "We're talking about self-worth . . . not self-worship!" When I speak to teens, I warn them that conceit is a strange disease that makes everyone sick—except the person who has it.

Encouraging your child to have good self-esteem does not mean you find ways to think he's superior to everyone else in the world. It doesn't mean that you teach your daughter that she'll never meet anyone prettier than she is (even though you may privately feel that way). Instead you seek to give them honest but humble views of themselves.

What makes teens feel good about themselves? In my survey these answers made the top five:

> Friends
> Compliments
> Good grades
> Sports
> Accomplishments/success

The top fifteen also included answers such as:

Liking myself
Going to church
Being with God
Praying
Taking with loved ones
Saying no to things that are wrong
Loving others and caring about them

Notice that none of these are material things. Way down on the list of answers came things like clothes, cars, and stereos. Despite the material temptations of this world, teens seem to understand that *things* just don't hit the spot, when it comes to creating self-esteem. Most of their answers focused on interpersonal relationships or their own ability to do things well.

Young people need to feel accepted, loved, and important, and friends and compliments make them feel this way, as do relationships with those at church and with God, talking with loved ones, and caring for others.

But teens also need a sense of personal accomplishment. The child who cannot achieve in some area will feel anything but special. She needs to know that someone notices her accomplishments and cares about them. Your daughter may not have a lot of friends, and she may not have numerous accomplishments. Brag about the ones she *does* have. Give her reason to feel good about herself, and you'll soon have more to share.

My sister Jeannie brags about her children. She will send my family copies of their grades, an article written about them, or any other smaller accomplishment. When her children saw the photocopies go out and heard her talk, they began to blossom. Help your child do the same.

Instead of buying their young people more new clothes, many parents need to brag about them, hug them, and tell them they are loved. When it came to describing the things that made them feel good about themselves, many teens listed parents/family behind accomplishments. Perhaps that's because they haven't received much affirmation within the family.

The pressures of the world try to tell us—and our children, "Buy this, and you will feel good." We may have fallen for the lie, but our teens have not. To meet their need for self-esteem, we must show our young people that we, too, understand that attention, accomplishments, and feeling special mean more than how much money you have, the way you live, or the clothes you wear. As our teens understand this better, they will respect those who come from the other side of town, even if they look, talk, and act differently. That will ready them for relating with a broad range of people in our diverse society.

I'm not advocating that you never allow your son to have clothes that fit in with the crowd, and the truth is if parents picked all the kid's clothes, he might not have any friends at all. Certainly a child should have some special outfits, but the teen who wants a fifty- or sixty-dollar pair of jeans should pay part of the price. Neither buy a child everything he wants nor deny him everything; find a balance.

Support and Rules.   Parents who want to develop self-esteem in their children need to love and support them, but they also need to set rules. Parents may avoid setting rules in one of two ways. A neglectful one lets her daughter run her own life, with little or no intervention; the mother becomes so involved with her own life that she never bothers to set rules. Permissive parents may give lots of love and support but let a child get away with anything. Either is the road to disaster.

I challenge you to provide your child with love by being a firm parent who is there. When a hug is needed, Dad, don't be too macho to reach out to your son. But also don't be afraid to set the rules. Sometimes young people break the rules because then they really get attention— even if it is the negative kind.

Support your child, give control by way of setting rules and sharing what they are. Your child will feel better and will make a stronger contribution to society if you do.

Why do teens run away from home? According to an article in *USA Today*, "Most share one thing: They believe, rightly or wrongly, their parents aren't interested in them."[1]

When Self-esteem Evaporates

If friends and compliments make a child feel good, it's not surprising that the opposite makes them feel lousy. Top on the list of things that made them feel bad was criticism/being teased.

If you give a person five compliments and one cutdown, which will remain in his mind five years later? Chances are, he'll remember the thing that stopped him, hurt him, or embarrassed him. Children are no different. They remember the negative, too. Events that are swept out of a parent's mind may remain with a child, if she sees them as put-downs, expressions of disappointment, or signs that her parent is angry.

Even when you feel tired, remain gentle with your children. After a long week at work, remember to be thoughtful and considerate.

This is an area in which I have difficulty gaining control. All week long, I speak to people, counseling couples with marital problems, talking to students who feel depressed, and so on. On Friday night, when I reach my own door, I feel drained. All I want to do is hug my wife and have fun with the kids, because I missed them. But as I walk in the door, what happens?

Two of the kids are upstairs, fighting. The third is in the other room, screaming and yelling with a friend. My wife, Holly, is upset because the pot roast just burned in the oven, and she couldn't find the video I wanted at the video store—it was all sold out.

After three seconds at home, I begin to wonder if I'd be better off three thousand miles away, in a school, among strangers.

Unlike last week's audience, the kids don't give me a standing ovation. They don't ask me to sign one of my books or tell me my words are the best they've ever heard. I've been gone all week, and they're ticked off because of it. They can't seem to admit that they missed me and hated my being gone. So they fight.

It's easy for me to explode, yell, and make them feel terrible. After all, I'm tired, irritable, and sick of being on a plane.

If I respond the way I feel, what message do I give my kids? While I was away, I called home every day, saying how much I missed them; but here I am home, and it's not the dad they want. When I yell at them, they think, *He really doesn't care.*

If I react in anger, after a while I have to get back with my kids and open their spirits. I need to ask their forgiveness, hug them, wrestle with them, and do whatever I can to let them know I *do* love and care about them. I ask you to regroup as well, when you goof up. It's really not that hard, and it brings you much closer.

The Importance of Relationships

The other things that made teens depressed included:

Bad grades
Having problems with parents
Failing at something
Being left out
Bad looks
Being overweight
No boyfriend or girlfriend
Losing at sports
Being yelled at
Being dumb

Note that none of these have to do with materialism. Just as with the things that made them feel good, these teens focused on the relationships that made them feel bad.

Notice that "having problems with parents" appeared on that list. When they don't admit that arguments with Mom and Dad upset them, your sons and daughters may just be hiding their real emotions. That's why it's so vital for parents to maintain rapport with their children.

When your child is happy, loving, and easy to be around, that's *not* the time she needs you most. When she acts irritable, quiet, shy, and your intuition says she's hurting inside, she desperately needs you. She may not seem in a mood to talk, but you have to be there for her. Ask her where she hurts, but spend most of your time listening, once she starts to open up. Become her encourager. Remember, when they're easiest to be around, they need us the least; and when they're hardest to be around, they need us the most.

Give Your Child Strength

Achievement is important to self-esteem, but sometimes it doesn't play a big role in a teen's life. No one will always be liked, achieve the greatest success, or receive all the prizes. Life doesn't work that way. So prepare your child for the tough times. Here are a few guidelines.

Teach Your Child to Build Strong Relationships. Give your child
a gift: Teach the tricks of the trade in making and keeping friends. It's
important to your son or daughter to make and keep relationships with
others.

> Psychologists estimate that between 5 and 10 percent of the
> children in elementary school classes are without friends. Several
> studies show that disliked children are more likely to have trouble
> in school than more popular students are. . . . The drop-out rate for
> rejected children was more than seven times that of popular chil-
> dren. Other studies suggest that rejection in the early grades is
> related to juvenile delinquency, criminal behavior and mental ill-
> ness later on.[2]

If parents don't pick up on rejected children's problems, they feel
totally left out in the cold. When no one at school cares about them, they
won't want to stay there—thus the high drop-out rate among them. When
even the people at home don't provide love, where can young people
turn?

Parents, become a refuge for your children. When others cut them
down or make fun of them, yours can be the loving arms that wrap around
them. Let your sons and daughters know that even if parents are old-
fashioned, they can make young people feel so special that it doesn't
much matter if the world hates them.

God wants us to experience that kind of love, even when we're rejected. He tells us the way to destruction is wide, easy, and takes no
effort on our part. But the way to truth, the way to God, through His Son,
Jesus, is narrow. Many people will reject you if you stand up for Him,
but when the rest of the world rejects you, Jesus will still love you.

Teach Your Child to Do What's Right. When I speak to teens, I
tell them that doing what is right—honoring your parents, wearing your
seatbelt, and sticking up for the unpopular kid—will never place you in
the majority, but it will put you in demand.

I want your daughter to be the most sought-after girl in school because
she handles herself in the right way and doesn't give in to pressure. I
want your son to have boys and girls wanting to hang around him, not
only because he's the one who's cool, but because he stands up for the

less privileged or less than beautiful. People will know that he stands up for ideals and doesn't take advantage of others. They will know he's saving himself for marriage.

I want your teens to establish good behavior patterns—such as not going to parties where there are illegal drugs or accepting the role of designated driver for teens who want to drink illegally, because such behavior would endorse these actions.

Give your children a vision for doing the right thing. Sometimes it may be hard, but in the end, they will have respect from others—and they may even become popular because people know what they stand for.

I close most of my assemblies with this sentence: "If you stand for what's right, you'll never be in the majority, but you will be in demand."

Teach Your Child It's Okay to Fail. No one feels good about failure. But teach your child that everyone does it. At the height of his career, Babe Ruth struck out more than anyone else!

Have you taught your son that failure is part of life? Have you told your daughter that the only true failure is the person who never tries because she might goof up? Teach your children that getting something wrong is merely another way of trying it.

By allowing your son to fail, you'll give him stamina. Tell him about the thousands of marriages that are still alive and going strong because husbands and wives have had disagreements and worked through and beyond them. Teach your daughter to forgive, forget, and move forward. Become your teen's greatest model.

Help Your Child Avoid the Trap of Depression. You know how it is: Your youngest child has just said something incredibly cute. You laugh. What she did was spontaneous, off the wall, accidental . . . and funny.

But the laughter that makes you happy may make your child sad. She doesn't understand that you're not laughing *at* her.

For several years now, we've worked to make our children understand that we're not laughing at them in such circumstances. We've tried to help them appreciate that it's great to make people laugh, because you're making the world a brighter place.

Where once my children used to feel frustrated and angry and would begin to cry when we'd laugh at something silly that they'd done, they've gained in understanding. But lots of that has come because I've been careful not to laugh as often or spontaneously. I always make a point to let them know that I'm laughing at them in love. By letting them know that what they did was cute, I assure them I was not putting them down.

The *Dallas Morning News* reported, "Two recent surveys of nearly 3,300 Dallas Independent School District high school students found that roughly two of every 10 respondents were moderately to severely depressed. . . ." According to the survey, minority students were more commonly depressed than whites. It concluded, "Many students don't feel they have control of their lives. If there's one message that the psychologist and social workers hope the public will glean from the surveys, it is that adults need to take time to listen to the young people in their lives."[3]

Dare we wait for some other adult to listen to our children first? No, let's take the time to listen to our own children. By doing so, we'll keep them from the lifelong affliction of depression.

One day, after an assembly, a girl shared with me that her mother had died, and she needed a friend.

I didn't know what to say, but that didn't matter. I held her lightly, and we cried together. Even though no words could solve her problem, I was there, and I cared. Other teens looked on, thinking that we were weird, but it didn't matter.

No one had ever told this girl that she was still in the grieving process. She felt she was wrong because she couldn't accept her new stepmom. When I told her that it was all right for her to hurt at the loss of her mom, it helped a lot.

According to one survey, 54 percent of all kids want their parents to "be more interested in the things that they care about. About 59 percent of the 8,000 fifth- to ninth-graders surveyed say their moms hug or kiss them daily. Only 39 percent of the same kids say their fathers do."[4]

Moms, Dads, are you getting involved with your children? Do you share things together? Do you have hugs every day? Children need their parents to care enough to share, listen, hurt with them, wrestle, and kiss. We can't just do it once and expect them to hold onto that for four months. Do it daily, over and over again, so your children will believe you're there all the time for them.

Action Plan for Parents

1. Make a list of the things that you know build up or tear down your children. Talk with them to discover areas you've missed. Together come up with a plan for encouragement and another that will help reduce the hurt. Share ways they build you up and tear you down.

2. After you've talked to your children, look for ways in which you've made them feel good or bad about themselves. How have you been supportive? Do you need to ask your child's forgiveness in any area? Have you discovered places in which you need to become more sensitive?

3. How much time do you spend with your child? Can you improve the ways you encourage and support her? Let her know you are willing to help her through problems. Show her that you will be there, no matter what.

4. How does school make your child feel about himself? Together with him, develop strategies that will help him feel more positive about his accomplishments and personality.

5. Have you given your child strength in the four ways listed in this chapter? Go over them again and evaluate what you've communicated to your teen. How can you build further strength?

5

WHAT ARE MY PROBLEMS?

Because I used an anonymous survey, students could freely fill in their deepest concerns and worries. One interesting statistical chain appeared. When I asked teens about their greatest problems, they placed school/grades/homework above peer pressure and drugs. But when I asked about the largest pressures put upon teens by their peers and the largest problem that America faces today, drugs and alcohol shot up to the top ratings.

The drug war doesn't seem to let up. A survey of eight- to twelve-year-olds reported on in *USA Today* said that drugs were the number-one problem.[1] These are second through sixth graders, not the junior-high and high-school students I surveyed. In my survey, 16.9 percent named drugs as their greatest problem, with alcohol following at 15.5 percent—together that means 32.4 percent of our students feel pressured to use addictive substances.

Pressure to Achieve

Though I'm not discounting the influence drugs have on our young people, 36.2 percent of the teens polled labeled the pressure surrounding schoolwork one of their three largest problems. Some students have told me they were ready to commit suicide because they could not face Mom and Dad with the news that the college of their choice had not accepted them. Others cannot give their parents the news about a bad report card.

I'm not saying we should not encourage our children to achieve, but we need to be aware of the pains, frustrations, and worries that go with pressure to get good grades, be on a team, and maybe even hold down a job, too. They need to learn how to have a balanced life.

According to one study of middle-income families, the pressure to achieve may begin early—and it may end in burnout. Though the very young children whose parents pushed them to achieve learned to read numbers and letters earlier, they also became more nervous and less creative in the long run.[2]

Are you expecting your youngster to spend four or five hours a night on her homework? If she doesn't have a quiet room to do her work in, will even that help? Is it all necessary? Have you given her the opportunity to be a child?

If you have a strong concern for your child, wanting her to do well so that she has a happy life, that's fine. But deep down many parents want to have that daughter do well so they can brag to their friends about the great college she got into—and the impressive career she's headed for. How happy will the same parents be if they see her drop out of school because the pressure was too great? When a child has become a parental trophy, something's out of whack.

It's fine to brag about your children, but beware of making bragging a form of pressure. "More than 10% of [college] freshmen reported frequently 'feeling depressed,' compared with 8.2% in 1985."[3] Is the need to succeed really so great that we want our children to suffer emotionally?

A wise principal shared with me the last question he asks a prospective teacher. "I have a true or false question for you," he explains. "If you get it right, you get the job; and if you don't, you don't get the job, and I will call your college to make sure you never teach in this state. If that happens, you might as well just find another profession."

By then he has the prospective teacher's attention.

"The question is 'Is black white?' " the principal asks.

The teacher looks puzzled.

"Obviously," the principal finally admits, "that question was non-sense. What *was* important was this: I don't ever want you to put that kind of pressure to learn on our children. I want them to come to love to learn. I want them to enjoy life because they are in your presence for one thousand hours a year. I want them to be excited about expanding their minds and learning new facts, so they can apply the principles to everyday life.

"If you can make learning fun and not just a collection of facts surrounded by too much stress for kids to handle, I would be proud to have you on my staff and team."

Let's be careful how much pressure we put on our children. Maybe easing up and showing them how to have balance in their lives will be one of our greatest gifts to them.

Pressure to Use Drugs

In part perhaps teens emphasize drugs and alcohol as problems because they receive such great media attention. However, when my survey asked, "What are the three largest pressures put on you by your peers," well over 50 percent of the students admitted they felt pressure to abuse drugs or alcohol.

What message do we pass on to our teens about drug and alcohol abuse? A double one. California's biggest cash crop—marijuana—makes almost $1 billion dollars a year more than its biggest legal cash crop—milk and cream.[4] But the illegal crop still grows. In Ann Arbor, Michigan, possessing marijuana is a misdemeanor; and more often than not, the police do not even bother stopping small-time users, because such an arrest isn't worth the paperwork. Alcohol, the leading killer of teenagers, we soft-pedal even more:

> We teach our young people to drink at home, instead of encouraging them to say no.
> We tell teens not to drink and drive—implying that it's okay to drink.
> We say we're against drunk drivers, but we do nothing to convince the police to pick up kids driving away from a teenage booze party.

We ask the police to protect our homes, but when we want to drink, we expect them to look the other way.

We do nothing about cute beer commercials that show an adorable little puppy or beautiful horses. Why do the animals look so good? Because they don't drink the product they advertise! Do our teens know that?

On one hand we tell teens drinking is wrong, but simultaneously we undermine that belief. We artfully give them such mixed messages that it's no wonder our youngsters feel confused.

How confused are *we*? One beer-company spokesman claims, "The bottom line is, advertising doesn't cause a person to drink beer or not drink beer."[5] If he's right, why would a company spend millions of dollars to show beer commercials during the biggest football game of the year—the Super Bowl? Why would any business spend so much of its profits on advertising?

Many people want our children's money, hearts, and souls. Are we willing to fight for them? The battle is more real than we might imagine: "A fourth of students grades five through 12 think they can experiment with drugs without slipping into drug abuse, and the percentage rises the older a student gets," a survey says.[6]

The pressure doesn't ease up as they get older, either.

When a teen who doesn't drink on Friday night enters the locker room Monday morning, he might expect the conversation to go something like this: "Why weren't you there? What are you, some kind of sissy? Mr. Religion, over there in the corner."

"Come on, wise up and party down. What could it hurt?"

"My grandpa drank until he was ninety-seven. *He* died of old age."

Are we helping teens face that kind of pressure? Twenty percent of them named peer pressure as their greatest problem, and over fifty-six percent said either drugs or alcohol was one of the three greatest pressures they felt. When everyone at school says, "It's okay to do drugs and drink," you've got to give teens strong reasons to fight against that attitude.

Remember, in many schools, the people everyone looks up to may be some of the heaviest drinkers. Athletes, the coolest guys they know, are often known as drinkers—by students, parents, and the community.

Eighty-eight percent of the 798 coaches surveyed by USA Today say alcohol is the greatest threat to their athletes. Six percent identified cocaine and/or crack as the major problem and one percent cited illegal steroids. Among black coaches surveyed, 31 percent consider hard drugs the biggest threat as compared to 5 percent of the white coaches. However, 63 percent of the black coaches listed alcohol as a bigger threat, as did 91 percent of their white counterparts.[7]

We've already seen that attitudes in the neighborhood will affect your children. Certainly teens don't come up with the drinking and dope habits from nowhere. Many see them at home—and pass what they've learned on to their friends.

By becoming active in the needs of the entire community—speaking out against drug use and encouraging those who need help to seek it—you can also begin to have an impact on the schools. But be aware that in order for students to take the danger seriously, both parents and schools will have to set standards and enforce them.

Take a stand—for the sake of your children!

Sexual Pressures

Though parents may remember the tough pressure their peers placed on them to have sex, often today's teen has to contend with more. Despite the deadliness of AIDS, increasing numbers of teens seem to make premarital sex part of their lives.

College women have reported, "I'm the only virgin on the entire floor of my dorm." Others have been virgins who made it their goal to lose their virginity. Why? Because of peer pressure! Many college students do not consider someone a desirable spouse if he or she has not had experience with sex. Young people badly want to fit in, even to the point of compromising their standards. The New York polling firm Audits and Surveys polled 1,300 high school students and 1,600 college students. They found that 57 percent of high-school students and 79 percent of the college students had lost their virginity.[8]

A Louis Harris poll reported: "54% of boys and 22% of girls in junior and senior high said they'd have sex with someone they loved. . . . 70% say girls should have the final say about having an abortion; 57% would advise a pregnant friend to have the baby. . . . 80% of all the kids feel pushed to obey their parents. What are the parents telling them to do?"[9]

It makes you wonder, doesn't it?

Again, realize that the ideas you have in your home and community have come into the schools.

What Can Parents Do?

If you feel concern about the level of sexuality expressed in your school system, and you want to know what's going on, begin by looking at how often you speak to your children about sex. Do they feel free to come to you with questions? Then consider the input the sex-ed teacher, your child's friends, and people from birth-control clinics have.

Correct, loving information is most likely to come from the home. If you want your child not to come away with the idea that wrong is right and right is wrong, he needs to hear what the Bible has to say and why God says wait until marriage. Let your child know that having sex has long-term consequences: the pain of feeling used, the horrors of post-abortion-stress syndrome, the influence old memories have on marital relationships. Provide facts that will help in decision making.

I'm not naive enough to believe that *no* teens will have sex before marriage, if only they hear of the dangers and God's way of abstinence, but does that mean I shouldn't help as many as possible discover these truths? So many people—parents, teachers, and school administrators—have a go-with-the-flow idea that says, "Teens will be teens, and you can't do anything about it." Maybe the sex-ed course your child has only mentions abstinence once in the entire year. If your child is out that day, she missed the message entirely.

I'm sure you don't want your child used and abused. You don't want a daughter who feels as if she's a pair of old shoes that have been on and off a boy's feet—and hates herself for that. You don't want a son who thinks that every girl is his right and he'll never need to settle down with one good, strong relationship. The sorrow that comes from such temporary relationships need not be part of your child's life.

But as long as parents omit talking about sex with young people, the teens will feel only the influences around them in the school and community. The streets are no place for a sex-education program.

Teach your son he's made in God's image; let your daughter know that God has a plan for her life and for marriage. Help them make commitments that last. By telling your children that sex within marriage is right, and sex outside that commitment is wrong, you give them important weapons in the battle against sexual pressures.

When it comes to answers about sex, let your children know you will always be there for them. Then follow through on that promise. Don't just tell your daughter, "I'll be here if you need me," once, when she's thirteen. Say it over and over again and teach her that by your actions. Establish habits and patterns of trust. Make yourself her number-one friend and resource. As you show that you care for her by daily listening, talking, and helping her find solutions, you'll build a trust that she'll still have when she's thirty.

As you make this part of your life-style, you'll become one of those parents who can talk to teens and relate well to them. Still, it's not enough just to talk. Set the standard *and* the example. Over and over tell your child, "You can say no to anything, with God's help and my support." Then show your child what it's like to say no—with your own life.

Family Pressures

Almost 20 percent of the students I polled named parents/family as one of the three greatest problems they faced.

Now we're not talking about something that's far away. Family problems hit both teens and parents right where they live. Even good, caring parents can have trouble with their teens. So let's look at a few practical ideas about how you can be there for your child.

Make Family Time a Priority. How much time do you spend with your family? According to one report, although some Americans felt concern about family values, many more felt concerned about providing for their families. When asked to choose between a job that would take them away more and time with the family, two-thirds would opt for the job. Cutting back on income was not really more important to these parents than the family values they felt concerned about.[10]

Recently I talked to some parents who felt angry with their sixteen-year-old son. They just couldn't seem to get through to him. As we shared dinner, they told me they'd simply left him home because he wouldn't even talk to them.

"One of the greatest things you could do," I shared, "is to let him know you'd be willing to give up this dinner engagement, a vacation, or other plans, because his happiness is so important to you. By doing that, you can *show* him, not just tell him, that you mean business with his life. Let him know you want his best and do not want to add to his problems."

Remember, even if your son is the 225-pound linebacker on the high-school football team, he wants to be able to talk to you about the issues that are on his high priority list. Though he may appear strong, on the inside he still needs his mom and dad.

When your son spends more than six hours of the day in a world that pressures him to drink, smoke, and steal, he needs the support of a good homelife in order to keep strong in the temptations of life. Provide a resting place, a quiet, resource-filled ground in which he can prepare for the next day.

More than all the material things in the world, your child wants a happy family life. That means more than winning the lottery, owning a fancy home, or having all the dream vacations in the world.

The Horror of Abuse

Not every teen has the kind of solid, supportive family that can provide the kind of care I'm advocating. When I asked young people if they'd ever been abused sexually, emotionally, or physically, many responded that they had been—and for some the abuse had not yet ended.

Look at some horrifying statistics concerning sexual abuse:

> A survey of American women who said they had been sexually abused before age 18 indicated that 29 percent were first abused by their biological fathers and 31 percent by another relative, *Glamour* magazine reports. Only 4 percent said the abuse was by a stranger. The magazine estimates that more than one out of three adult women and one out of seven adult men have been abused before age 18.[11]

Abuse is not something that usually occurs outside the family; it's a hurt that often sticks with our basic living structure: Mom, Dad, and the kids.

The parent or other adult who inflicts such abuse makes his own hurts apparent. Surely he lacks wisdom, love, and understanding. As a result, he also causes the abused child to become tied up in anger and pain. When she's forty-five, she may still be dealing with that. Sometimes the memories last for a lifetime, if professional counseling is not found.

No matter what the abuse—sexual, emotional, or physical—the child needs help. She may not be able to express the pain that has become a regular part of her homelife. Caring, observant adults need to see when a neighbor's child is scarred or bruised or seems to suffer from continual emotional pain. Relatives, too, need to keep an eye out for their extended families.

What a shame that so many cases of abuse go unreported. Are we afraid to help a hurting child? Do we look the other way at church, in the workplace, and in our neighborhoods? If so, we've become guilty of a sin of omission:

The Sin of Omission

It's not the thing you do,
  it's the thing you leave undone
That gives you such a heartache
  at the setting of the sun.

The tender word forgotten,
  the note you did not write.
The flowers you never sent,
  are your haunting ghosts at night.

The stone you might have lifted
  from a brother's way:
The bit of heartfelt counsel
  you took no time to say.

The loving touch of hand,
  the gentle winning tone
Which you took no time nor thought for
  you had troubles of your own.

Those little acts of kindness
  so easily out of mind,

Those chances to be angels
which we too seldom find.

They come in night and silence
each sad reproachful wraith.
When hope is faint and flagging,
and a chill is on our faith.

For life is all too short
and sorrow all too great,
To embrace a slow compassion
that tarries till too late.

No, it's not the thing you do,
it's the thing you leave undone
That gives you such a heartache
at the setting of the sun.

MARGARET E. SANGSTER

Because of our own unwillingness to take action, are we condemning a child to the kind of pressure abuse causes in a family? How can a child who experiences deep hurt within the home say no to drugs, alcohol, and sex? When life looks hopeless, those things seem to relieve the pain. Unless a caring adult comes alongside that youngster to provide hope, the same sad story may repeat . . . and repeat . . . and repeat.

Teens see the violence on TV; they hear about it all around them. They need to know that life doesn't have to be that way. Unless we start sowing seeds of hope, we'll be condemned to a society even more filled with abuse.

Family violence is spreading rapidly—in our own communities. Unless *we* act, who will stop it? Don't be just a reader, become a doer. Learn the signs of abuse and help a child whose family is wrapped up in violence. Fight against pornography, media that would demean the family, and other signs of poor family life. Give the next generation a chance.

Let's start a groundswell of ideas that teach our children: People are important and should not be used or abused.

Pressure to Fit In

When it comes to fitting in, kids may express their need in many ways: They may describe their desires and fears about "making friends," "not being picked on," "growing up," or "shyness." All of these have to do with being part of a group.

The desire to be part of a group is normal; every human needs companionship. Help your child discover that you don't need to be the brightest, prettiest, or most talented student to feel good about yourself and make friends.

What kind of friends does your child bring home? As a parent, you can probably see a lot. My mom could always spot the bad pennies. I might have thought that the "good" kids were boring and didn't offer the thrills that other kids provided, but in the long run I can say my mother was absolutely right about every single case, and I'm sorry I didn't listen to her.

Don't try to make your son fit into the football team if his thing is debating. Don't force your daughter to play the flute if she's crazy about joining the hockey team. It just doesn't work like that. Together you need to discover the strong points your child has and suit actions to talents. By helping your children gain confidence in their natural abilities, you help them feel good about themselves.

Encourage your children. The pains, difficulties, and challenges will come. Teach them to be overcomers!

Action Plan for Parents

1. How do you think you have placed pressure on your child to achieve? Talk to your child. How does he or she perceive your pressure? Have you unconsciously pushed your son or daughter to succeed? If so, what can you both do about it?

2. Talk to your child about the pressures to use drugs and alcohol. How much pressure is in the school? The community? How does your child respond to it? Can you help in any way?

3. How much does your child know about the dangers of drug use? How has this affected his or her opinion of drugs? Together can you learn more about these dangers?

4. How often do you talk to your child about sex? Is it a lecture or

a conversation with give and take? How can you communicate better on this subject?

5. What are the signs of physical, emotional, and sexual abuse? Magazine articles, newspaper reports, and books may help you become aware of family-violence patterns. Discover what local resources are provided, so you can help an abused child and his or her family turn their lives around. Check local listings of family counseling, look for church-related services, and read up on active groups in your area. Attempt to discover something of their beliefs before you recommend them.

6. Have you set apart a regular sharing time for family? If you don't have such times, what has kept you from them? Begin to plan changes in your family life that will help you share together.

7. Have you made special plans that your children could take part in? Together decide on a vacation schedule, start a family project that helps others, or develop some goals you can share. Make certain you plan to spend time together, discussing, considering, and working out any bugs in your planning.

8. What kind of pressure does your child feel to fit in with others? How does he or she handle it? Are there ways you can help?

9. Sit down with your child and discuss his or her natural abilities. Are these the things he or she is doing now? Would your son like to become involved in something new that he's never tried? Is your daughter involved in activities she doesn't really like but feels she must continue? Together you may need to plan some changes. Encourage your child to try new things and not hold on to activities that do not suit his or her abilities.

10. What kind of friends do your children bring home? Are they good influences or bad ones? Do your children seek to help their friends or pick up bad habits from them? What lessons can you learn about your son or daughter's desire to fit in? About his or her abilities?

6
WHOM DO I LOOK UP TO?

Having problems is a part of life, and teens face just as many difficulties as adults do—though teens' troubles often seem smaller to adults. How young people feel about themselves and their parents will have a great deal to do with where they go to get advice and help in adversity.

Whom Do I Turn To?

How do your children find out about sex, drugs, how to fit in, or what is cool? When they feel upset, depressed, or afraid, whom do they turn to? If your fourteen-year-old son's best friend is talking about suicide, can he tell you? What if your daughter's best friend in math class has confided that she's abused at home? Your daughter promised not to tell, but should she keep silent?

You need to ask yourself, *Are my children coming to me or going to someone else?* Every child wants some straight, loving answers. Can you provide them? Or are you and your teen just too far away from each other?

Friends

According to my survey, 66.9 percent of all teens go to their friends for advice. Where do most teens learn about life? According to one survey, it's probably from the media:

> 703 student leaders responding to a USA Today poll: listen to music an average of 3.8 hours a day, watch TV 2.6 hours, are on the phone 2.1 hours. And they average two hours a night on homework. That's 10.5 hours a day. They also see 2.8 movies and 7.5 videos a month, read 2.5 books a month, 4.2 newspapers a week. Girls listen to music four hours a day, boys 3.3 hours. [1]

When you leave your children to their friends, you'll find they often make decisions based on the input of MTV, the latest sitcom, or the newest movie. Teens lack your experience in life. They don't have adults' wisdom and knowledge. Even the best teen in the world can't know what an adult knows.

Family

But the statistics on friends do not mean that teens turn only to their friends. I asked for three sources of advice, and family members' percentages appeared significantly:

Parents	39.9%
Mom	17.0%
Relative/family	14.5%

Looking at these, you quickly understand that family life can have a strong impact on a teen's decisions. Don't fall for the lie that you can't influence your teens!

Though your teens may turn first to friends, they don't have to take their advice. When they come to you, it may be because they want a broader opinion. Remember, too, the advice of Proverbs 22:6: "Train a child in the way he should go, and when he is old he will not turn from it." Though your son or daughter may not follow your advice today, remain consistent, and the fruit of your labors may appear somewhere down the line.

Help your teens overcome the input of the media by starting to set trends. Encourage them to read instead of watching television. That way they'll actively use their brains instead of seeking passive entertainment.

When my kindergartners come home, the first thing they want to do is turn on the television. After all, their friends will be talking about the cartoons tomorrow, and they want to be part of that. But my wife, Holly, and I have set severe limits on what they can watch. Because so many of the shows have heavy violence, we don't allow them to watch much. For our children the Ninja Turtles are out, as are all the superheroes who beat up others in the name of justice and the many programs that include witchcraft.

What *can* our kids do instead? One thing is to become unusual by spending some time with Dad.

Look at the sad statistics about father-child relationships in America. "The average five-year-old spends only 25 minutes a week in close interaction with his father, according to one study. The same child spends 25 hours a week in close interaction with the TV."[2]

I don't like the odds of twenty-five hours of TV to twenty-five minutes with Dad. What are my children learning from the television? I've noticed that, when a commercial comes on, even if my kids are in another room, they come to listen. The advertisers know just how to grab their attention, and the increased volume draws them to the commercial. I'd like my children to have more than an ad mentality.

But before we can limit what our kids watch, we need to become aware of our own television habits and make some changes, if necessary. For example, many people may feel daytime television is safer than the prime-time shows. But before you encourage your youngsters to turn on the TV, consider these statistics:

> Daytime television contained 50% more sexual references than prime time, the report said. 33 instances per hour versus 23. Daytime serials were the chief repository (35 instances per hour), said the report, followed by theatricals (30), made-fors (24), sitcoms (24) and prime time serials (21).[3]

Several times I have watched soaps, and what I viewed there caused me to come to this decision: I will not allow soap operas in my home, even for five minutes. How can parents think this is safe watching for their children, when the hero or heroine of the story gets out of trouble one day, only to get into it again the next? You'll see the hero in bed with his wife, her best friend, or someone else. Do my children need this message of promiscuous sex? No!

Parents, you need not eliminate all television watching from your schedule, but you can make good choices and teach your children to do the same. Use some of that found time to talk to your children, take part in new activities with your teens, and make family life creative and exciting.

Over twenty percent of the teens I surveyed reported that they went to siblings for advice, and another 14.5 percent went to other family members. While that's encouraging, it's hard for youngsters with extended families who live miles and miles away to have the kind of input and support that could help them make wiser decisions. With smaller immediate families, they have more limited resources.

When your child has a bad week, it's important for her to know that she can go to her siblings. One way my wife and I teach our children to encourage one another is through a game we play at mealtime. We pick out one family member, and each person has to say, "I love you because _____" and fill in the blank with the reason. The complimented person has to say, "Thank you, _____," filling in the blank with that person's name. Use this in your own family to teach your children how special and unique they are and to help them love and cherish one another.

When I was a child, I didn't appreciate my younger brother, Dale. Though my mom tried to get me to play with him and accept him, I wouldn't. Dale was three years my junior and nearly as strong as I. He was twice as good as I was in most sports, and I didn't want him to outshine me. So instead of building a friendship, I spent all my time working at being better than he was and at becoming more popular than Dale. Today, though we are very close, I still regret the wasted years, when I could have helped him and been friends with him.

If I see my children pick on one another, it hurts, because I know what I lost with my brother. I don't want them to experience my disappointment.

Other Resources

What else did young people list as decision-making resources? Some said they talked to teachers or a boyfriend or girlfriend. Quite often below that was pastor/priest or God.

How sad that we haven't taught each of our children to go to God first and seek the answers in His Word. He has the answers, and He promises to help us.

"Delight yourself in the Lord and he will give you the desires of your heart" (Psalm 37:4). Who wouldn't want the desires of his heart? We need to teach our children that God loves them more than anyone else could. We can teach them to look to God, trust in Him, and seek His advice. He should be their first choice as a confidant: "It is better to take refuge in the Lord than to trust in man" (Psalm 118:8).

One speaker gave a program in a school that asked him back a year later. But before they would let him do another speech, the principal made one request: "Please don't mention God this time."

The speaker felt surprised, because he had not openly mentioned his faith in Jesus. He had only generally referred to it.

"Okay," he told the principal. "I'll make a deal with you. I will not mention Jesus, faith in God, or our need to lean on Him and go to Him for advice."

The principal began to smile, until he heard the rest of the deal.

"I'll not mention God or Jesus if *you* will promise me one thing."

"What's that?"

"That you will be here for those kids 100 percent of the time, when they are hurting—that's twenty-four hours a day. Make certain your phone is never busy, because I have taught kids that if they go to God in prayer, He will never be too busy for them. Make sure that you tell the most unpopular kids in the school, the most unloved, and the biggest troublemaker that you will be their best friend. You will never leave them and will always listen to them. I want you to visit them daily and be willing to die for them.

"If you'll do this, then I will not mention God. I won't have to."

The principal got the message. "I tell you what I think we should do. You go ahead and do what you normally do. Don't alter your message one bit. Keep bringing God in here. Now I see why they appreciate you so much."

Who else can offer you a deal like God's? Teach your teens to turn to Him.

A Reason to Hope

When I see the kind of answers most teens give me about the people they turn to, I feel optimistic. They have some good support, if they are just willing to use it. Encourage your teen to take part in this kind of system. Why should yours be the child who answered "no one else/ myself"? For 6.9 percent, their own advice seemed the only option.

To young people like this, we need to reach out with the news that someone *does* care. How often does it take a crisis to show people that those around them would have been happy to help—if they had only known about the problem. Encourage your teens and their friends to learn to share with some of these people. If they can't go to Mom and Dad, maybe an aunt or uncle, a teacher or advisor can offer the badly needed help. Give them the courage to reach out, and youngsters can find help.

Who Are My Heroes?

One way we can see what's inside our children's minds is to take a look at the people they look up to. When we asked for three heroes in teens' lives, athletes rated high, but so did parents, friends, and siblings. In several schools, Dad was number one, and Mom number two. But at the least, parents held the third or fourth spot. Even when athletes, actors, or friends rated higher than parents, it became obvious that many kids would turn to their parents, because these quickly obsolete, distant people could not have an intimate impact on their lives.

Though our statistics do not show it, God or Jesus often made it near the top, too.

Do you help your children have the right kind of heroes? *You* don't have to fill the top slot in order to feel confident that your teens are making good choices. Get your children excited about the positive character qualities in their heroes. Encourage your daughter to look at the life-style of that sports star she'd like to emulate. Is this the way she'd like to live? Does that kind of life-style honor God?

If you encourage your children to put God first, they'll probably know what is right and wrong and how to successfully make many of life's tough decisions. They'll have help right at hand when they need it.

When your teens look up to a hero who has natural talents way beyond their own, they may feel discouraged. If the goal this person reached is way beyond their ability to succeed, your youngsters will feel defeated when they realize they'll never achieve greatness. Perhaps it's more realistic to look for heroes in athletes and musicians, relatives and friends who live nearby. By seeing them up close, your teens can better learn how to emulate their skills and efforts.

Don't just stop there. When I see exciting stories about teens who do wonderful things, I tell my kids about them. Recently I shared the story of a state-champion wrestler who only has one leg. I know that on days when my kids are having it tough, they can emulate this person who has overcome difficulties. Though they may never face his physical challenge, they can see the small things in their lives as just that and feel that they, too, can overcome big challenges.

If you mention a hero to your child, you may never know his or her entire life story. Or you may not be able to endorse that person's whole life-style. But do point out the heroic qualities. Focus on things your child can do, too. This does not necessarily include looks or specific talents, such as coordination, sporting abilities, or academic skills. Your child has his or her own God-given talents. Your daughter may never be able to be a tennis pro, and your son may never be a chess champion, but maybe they can learn from the lives of such people. Focus on character qualities you'd like to see your child develop.

For example, 6.8 percent of our students surveyed reported that they admired Michael Jordan. Now most teens will never be able to emulate his sports skills, but they can learn from his other qualities. He has stated he will not take part in booze or cigarette commercials. Because he knows he's a hero to many young people, he wants to live up to that role. I admire him for the integrity he has shown and his willingness to take on a difficult job—being a hero to millions of kids.

On the other hand, as I write this, Magic Johnson's story of contracting the HIV virus has hit the media. So far, his only advice has been to encourage teens to have safe sex. He has not mentioned a word about the wrongs and pains of premarital sex or the need for abstinence. At the same time, Wilt Chamberlain is making millions on his autobiography, in which he brags about having sex with over twenty thousand women. I can't look up to him anymore as a hero or a role model, and my kids know it.

You and I have to point out where these public figures are wrong. Our children deserve our honesty and courage in this area.

I keep a file of heroes. From time to time, I can bring it out and share with my children the extraordinary things other people are doing or the ways in which they use their God-given talents.

Look for the stories of average people who have done amazing things and begin your own file. As you discover good character qualities in these people, you can pass them on to your teens.

Whom Does Your Teen Admire?

Discover, too, what people your child looks up to. What qualities do these people have? When your son looks up to rock stars, is it because all his friends do, and he wants to be part of the crowd? Does your daughter *really* admire Madonna? Does she know about the video "Justify My Love," which portrayed so many sexual acts and fantasies that even MTV banned it? Can she understand that the sort of life-style portrayed there will only hurt her in the end?

Perhaps you will not turn your teen away from admiring the latest singer. If not, take courage in the fact that most such stars are just a fad. Bring real heroes alongside the ones she sees on TV or in the videos. Help her learn that real heroes have long-term goals and strong moral values. In the end, she'll begin to see what she really needs to look up to.

Action Plan for Parents

1. Whom do your teens turn to for advice? Why? If they do not seem to turn to you, begin to identify ways in which you can support your children. Are the people they go to giving good advice? Don't be jealous of someone who is doing your child a good turn by providing a solid moral base and good actions.

2. What kind of impact does TV have on your child? What example have you set? Do you need to make changes in your own viewing? How can you help your child make wise choices in choosing television shows? Together come up with a plan.

3. If each of you eliminates some television time from your schedules, will you have more family time? What can you do that will be exciting for you and your teens? Get together with your teens and discuss what you'd like to share together.

4. How can you encourage your children to support and help one another? How would they like to be supported? Can they help you come up with some areas for improvement?

5. Do your children turn to God for help? If not, why not? If so, how has He helped them? Spend some family time discussing the impact God can have on decision making and how you know when you have made a good decision. Do they ever wake up and find you on your knees, praying or reading the Bible?

6. Whom do your teens look up to? Ask your children to list some heroes. What have they done that is admirable? How have they failed? Does failure in one area of life mean that you should not admire that person? If not, what does it mean?

7. Go through some magazines and newspapers, looking for stories of local heroes. What have they done that you can admire? Have they fallen short in some way? Look also at stories of people who are shown as being admirable, but whom you cannot admire. Why can't you agree with the article? Share some of these stories with your teen and encourage him or her to start his own file. Spend some time together discussing the people you look up to.

7

WHAT AM I LEARNING FROM MY PARENTS?

While parents worry about what the school teaches their children, they unconsciously model a whole way of life: teaching teens some good things—and some bad ones.

To see what teens have learned at home, I asked a broad range of questions. I wanted to discover what parents and teens did—and how those teens felt about it.

Can Teens Talk to Parents?

I wanted to know how teens interrelate with their parents, so I asked. What can they share with them, and what topics do they avoid? The responses were mostly pleasantly surprising.

Over half the teens reported they could share in the areas of drugs, dating, emotions, alcohol, school, and pressures. School came in highest, at 86.2 percent. Once dating, drugs, and emotions came up for discussion, the statistics dropped into the seventies, and in some schools the ability to share emotions only reached 50 percent.

However, in a world with rampant sexually transmitted diseases, only

49.3 percent of the students I surveyed could discuss sex with their parents.

Barriers to Sharing

Why don't some teens share with their parents? Is it because their parents won't listen? Not in most cases. Only 4.3 percent specifically reported this fear. The top six concerns were:

> They don't understand
> Embarrassment
> I don't want a lecture
> I'm scared/I'm shy
> I don't know what their reaction will be
> I don't want to be punished

Often teens flip-flopped the first and second answers.
  Other objections included:

> I don't want them angry
> I do not talk to them about anything
> There is no time
> They won't listen
> They won't trust me anymore
> We don't get along
> I am ashamed
> They will laugh at me
> They will gossip

An even more disturbing line of answers included:

> My parents don't care
> I may get a friend in trouble
> My parents will hate me
> They will worry
> I hate to hear them cry
> I have no respect for my parents
> They are not honest with me

They will think I'm weak
I don't trust them

All these portray a lack of support and communication. In some cases, children so fear their parents that they can't seem to share. They may not want to experience embarrassment, or they may avoid having their parents come down hard on them, but both stem from fear. Something is lacking in their relationship. Later we'll discuss how you can improve communication and support in your family. Remember, you may be trying hard to communicate to your children, but if they perceive that you are too busy or don't care or that work comes first, that's what's real in their minds.

The Messages Teens Receive

In many ways how much teens will share depends upon the verbal and life-style messages they receive from parents. Though you may speak one message, they will respond to your actions, if they differ from your words. Parents who want to communicate well with their children will make an effort to do what they say. Integration of word and deed is so important!

Let's look at some of the messages teens receive.

Be a Success

When I asked teens about the greatest pressures they faced, school/grades/homework came in at the top of the list. So perhaps it should not surprise us that 57.8 percent of the students I surveyed also labeled that the greatest pressure put on them by parents. The rest of the pressures on the list came in with only a fraction of the votes that schoolwork got.

It's not wrong to want your child to do well in school—you need to encourage that. But keep the pressure realistic. Do you demand excellence—or near perfection—from your teen? Remember, if you turn the pressure on too high, you may get an awful surprise.

A few years ago a Dallas suburb experienced a rash of teen suicides. These were not underprivileged children. Those who took their lives came from houses with perfect yards, watering systems, three-car garages, and so on. You name the toy, and those teens had it.

After the suicides, people began to ask, "How could this happen? These kids had it all; didn't they know that their parents would do anything to keep them happy?"

Maybe so, but these teens who had too much also felt the pressure to live up to high parental standards. If they felt embarrassed to talk to their parents, afraid of ridicule or punishment, they could only explode from the emotional pressure.

Remember that your teen can only base his experiences on your family. In sixteen years, he hasn't seen everything. He doesn't know what other families do. If you don't communicate with him, he thinks that's the way life is. *No one cares what happens to me,* he may think. That's how teens become part of the suicide statistics.

No one is totally immune to the pain of a child who has not lived up to expectations, gotten involved in drug abuse, or somehow failed. But that's the time for parents to provide understanding, not more pressure. Ask yourself, *When do I need the most support—when things are going great or when I'm hurting?* It's the same with your kids!

When I drive by expensive homes in our town, and my children say, "I wish we lived there, Daddy," I remind them, "You don't see anyone playing in the yard. To make a house like that and pay for it takes a lot of time. Rarely can a daddy who does that spend a lot of time home with the kids."

How many huge homes have been built on a foundation of drug abuse, suicide, divorce, and families that have no relationships?

A little boy heard two rich boys bragging about their dads. Each had wealth and power, and the boys kept listing all the things they had.

"Yeah," the poor little boy said, "but while your dads have all those things, my dad is ready to play baseball with me right now." How much healthier is it for a boy to see his parents go off to work and come home happy, contented, and fulfilled than to have become part of a rat race that keeps them from enjoying their kids? Is the success worth it?

Realistic Pressure. Challenge your teens to do well in school, but keep it all in balance. Communication remains open if you encourage them instead of pressure them. Let them know they can tell you their problems at school, instead of making them feel they must earn your love by getting all A's or going to an Ivy League school.

Pressure can come in all shapes and sizes. I had a letter from one teen whose mother wanted her to stay at home all the time. The mother was ill and wanted help caring for the younger children in the family, but that was not really the reason she kept her daughter home. Because the mother had gotten pregnant as a teen, she feared her daughter would, too. To "protect" her teen, she pressured her into an unnatural social position.

Too much pressure can risk your child's mental health, causing shame, guilt, and anger. It can also lead to compulsive or addictive behaviors. Pain caused by pressure can last into middle age.

Don't make your child an achiever at the expense of her family life, marriage, and relationship with God.

Instead model balanced behavior. Start traditions, give hugs, and have some laughter in your home.

When I asked teens about the pressures parents put on them, I got this performance-oriented list:

Quit complaining
Keep morals
Don't steal
Go to church
Don't cheat
Respect your curfew
Be successful
Listen more
Talk more
Don't go to dances
Trust me
Let me earn your trust
Be kind
Don't swear
Drive carefully
Read the Bible
Be a good example
Don't be too emotional
Share your emotions
Baby-sit more

Be happier
Be honest
Don't listen to bad music
Spend your time wisely
Don't get caught up with peer pressure
Don't disappoint us
Open up more
Go to seminary
Don't play with guns
Don't watch too much TV
Have better manners
Eat right
Respect my car and leave it full of gas

Can anyone live up to all that? I doubt it! It sounds like a "should" list. Don't forget: If you don't "should" on me, I won't "should" on you!

So when your son drives your car home on fumes and gets it there—but without enough gas to get it to the gas station—understand that he's being a typical teen. He needs to learn how to handle the car better, but not by being screamed at!

In the midst of your concern for your teen's behavior, do you also want him to be happy, laughing, and honest? Do you model behavior that teaches him that, or are you habitually gloomy and scowling? When the phone rings, do you say, "If it's for me, I'm not here"? Are you courteous to people, caring about them first? Or do you push into line, in order to get your own way?

What you model to your teen will come out in his behavior. What you show to your daughter will come out in her life. Your teens watch, and they know you better than anyone else. If you say one thing and do another, they'll pick up on it and act on it. I tell parents, "You can con a con and fool a fool, but you can't kid a kid." Teens know when we walk our talk.

Do as I Say, Not as I Do

For years I've received letter after letter from hurting teens. They made me wonder how much teens trusted Mom and Dad. So I just had to ask, "Do your parents say one thing and do another?"

Almost 50 percent said yes!

Nearly half the young people in America seem to believe their parents are hypocrites in some area. But the good news is that over half of our young people believe their parents are honest, keep their commitments, and live by their words, promises, and convictions.

With the divorce rate at about 50 percent, I have to wonder if that's had a heavy impact on the hypocrisy teens see in parents' lives. Till death do us part?

Where did teens see their parents as hypocrites? Here are the top five areas:

> Going places with friends
> Alcohol
> Dating
> Smoking
> Doing things together

When I talked to teens, I discovered some of the specifics that made their parents hypocrites.

Going Places With Friends. Parents would tell their teens that some places were acceptable and others were not; they would tolerate some activities and not others. Then the parents would go out and do the very things they had forbidden their teens.

If you tell your teen not to go to a rough part of town and then visit there, why should he feel it's fair? When your back is turned, he may feel little guilt about going to that place. If you tell your daughter not to go to violent movies and then watch them on the video when she's not there, she'll understand that you're giving her a double message, and she may watch them on the sly, too.

When you say one thing and do the other, you cause your teens to lose respect for you. They will not want to come to you for advice if they know you don't live what you say.

Alcohol and Smoking. Alcohol topped many lists, or it was in second place. Though parents discourage teens from drinking, Mom and Dad need to drink to relax, celebrate, or have fun. From this, teens understand that to say it and play it are two different things. Teens want to relax and enjoy life more, so they follow the example their parents set.

It's the same with smoking. As parents abuse their bodies this way they negate the message: Smoking kills.

Dating. This answer surprised me. But many young people told me that their single parents told them to set high standards for dating—they outlined the qualities they should look for in dates—while they had a live-in boyfriend or girlfriend. Though these parents expected commitment from teens, they did not show them what it looked like.

Often teens are afraid of a live-in person. Many girls have written to me, complaining that they feared their mother's boyfriend. A boyfriend may look at the daughter improperly or make advances toward her. Several teens wrote of the sexual or emotional abuse heaped on them by their mothers' boyfriends.

Many years ago I noticed a girl who slept through most of my assembly program. When I asked about this later, someone told me she wanted to speak to me. That day we got together for a brief counseling session in the school. She shared how her mother's live-in boyfriend and her mother smoked marijuana at night, about five times a week.

The daughter, who had an allergy to the smoke, literally had to leave the house to do her homework in the car or at a friend's house. She'd return home about 2:00 A.M. No wonder she slept through my assembly!

Granted, not all cases are this extreme, but they do happen. If a parent models such behavior in front of a child, how can she have a leg to stand on when she speaks to her daughter about dating?

Who pays the price for an adulterous relationship? Though the parent may receive some hurt from it, far greater is the impact on the children involved.

> The impact of adulterous affairs on the children of the adulterers is profound. Children react negatively to reduced attentiveness by their parents, and to furtive discussions behind closed doors. Small children show anxiety when they perceive that the family is somehow disintegrating. . . . Parental affairs can markedly color a child's approach to adult behavior. A pattern of unreliability or of chronic distrust may result.[1]

When I speak to single parents who have live-in partners, I can almost always tie their children's behavior problems to the situation.

Extramarital relationships are not a good idea. They harm the parent and the child. When a sex counselor tells you an affair between two consenting adults who are in love and have a meaningful relationship will not hurt anyone, give yourself the freedom to disbelieve that statement. Look at what it can do to families, and look at the chances of a lasting marriage when a relationship begins that way:

> Close to half of American couples now are living together before they marry, but recent research shows that they are more likely to separate and divorce than couples who stop at the altar before they set up a joint household.
>
> According to the national survey, couples who lived together before they married were 40% more likely to be divorced within a decade than couples who did not.[2]

However, you don't have to have a live-in partner to lose your credibility on the subject of dating. What about parents who advise their children to choose their dates carefully—then berate a daughter because she isn't dating soon enough, often enough, or steadily enough? With those words she learns that her parents put upon her the same standard of self-worth that her peers do. The unspoken message is that if you don't have a lot of dates, there's something wrong with you.

Live up to what you say about dating. Don't make it a competition or a negative message. Instead teach your teens that it's a key to growth—and that you want the best for them.

Doing Things Together.   I've always said young people spell love the same way your spouse does: with four letters. I'm not talking about L-O-V-E, but T-I-M-E! Both your spouse and children know you care for them when you spend time with them.

Though teens rated doing things together number five, six, or seven in my survey, I think it is one of the most important areas in which you can concentrate, when it comes to family life.

Around our house, we have a little saying, "You don't just want to be a regular dad, do you?" When the children want me to do something for them—play a fifth game of checkers, throw a ball so they can get in some batting practice, or cut out paper dolls—they use this question. They know that regular dads don't get out of their chairs, when they feel tired, to wrestle with their kids, read to them, or go roller-skating. Many dads are too busy golfing, working, or spending time at something they love—other than the kids.

I don't want to be a regular dad—the kind who spends next to no time with his children—so I encourage my kids to ask me that question. It challenges me to become the best dad I can be.

Don't Get Me Involved

One interesting contrast was the difference in answers when asked, "How often do your parents know what you are doing on the weekends?" and, "Do you lie to your parents about what you do on the weekends?" Over 48 percent said their parents knew where they were at least 90 percent of the time. But at least 37 percent admitted that they did lie at least sometimes, and another 3.7 percent avoided the question altogether.

Almost three-quarters of our teens said that their parents asked about their weekend activities. Though only 23.7 percent said they had nothing to hide, 58.5 said they did not lie to their parents.

How can Mom and Dad discourage lying and encourage real communication with teens? I think part of it is to make a policy of involvement. Even though their teens lie, I suspect many parents have a pretty good idea what their young people are involved in. It's just easier to stay uninvolved, because then you don't have to deal with a confrontation.

Counselor David Mace identified three elements that make up marital success. I'd like to suggest that these can work in a parent-child relationship, too:

> Commitment to growth and change
> A system for regular communication
> Acceptance of conflict as normal and inevitable and the ability to learn to use it creatively[3]

Though conflict feels threatening, parents who do not learn to accept it and make the most of its creative powers will encourage their children to believe that they can demand anything they want of the world and gain it by deception when the world doesn't cater to their desires.

Become part of your teens' lives. Maybe your child is one of the nearly one-quarter of our teens who can be trusted. If so, you'll just be encouraged. If not, you may have an opportunity to give input into some critical issues. Even though you may increase the conflict for a while, you may ultimately improve the quality of your child's life.

Some teens can be trusted without supervision. If you have a sixteen-year-old who is always where he says he will be and shares freely with you, you may not need to do much. But don't let your fourteen- or fifteen-year-old go to a party at 7:00 P.M. and return at 12:00 A.M. without checking up on where he's going and what he's doing. At that age you need to demand that the party is chaperoned and has a closed-door policy. That means once the teens arrive they stay until the party is done. Know when the party ends, and be ready to offer a ride home, if necessary. I strongly believe that curfews should fluctuate according to the activity. Don't keep it at 12:00 A.M. if the dance ends at 10:00 P.M.

Why do teens try to hide their activities from parents? When I asked them this, they often responded that they felt it was important to be with this group—even though their parents wouldn't approve, and they knew it—and they felt a desperate need to be with these peers.

Wanting to be part of the crowd is a normal thing for teens—or adults. But discourage your teen from getting into a crowd that never informs parents what's going on. If necessary, make an effort to find out what's happening.

When I asked teens if their parents had ever called to see if parties were chaperoned, only about a quarter responded yes. Yet three-quarters had expressed interest in what teens did.

Why don't parents call? When I talk to them, they often tell me it's a matter of trust. But is it really trust—or ignorance? Do they simply want to avoid being involved? If you're one of the parents who wants to know what your teen is doing, don't be afraid to take an active role.

I'm not trying to say that no teen can be trusted. Surely that's not true. But by keeping in touch with what's going on in your child's life, you encourage her to become the honest, integrity-filled person you'd like her to be. You show that you do care, because you're willing to be a part of her life. Here's the rule to run by. First, tell your child what you *expect.* Then it's important that you *inspect* what she's doing. Your consistency and follow-through really prove your concern.

Building Better Communication

I'm not saying that being able to talk to a teen requires that you become a superparent. After all, look at some of the high numbers parents got on this survey. But almost all of us could use a little help in communication. Even the most firmly closed door can be opened, if parents consistently show that they care, are willing to spend time with teens, and will work through the rough spots. It takes a lot of dedication and time, but it *can* be done.

Let's look at a few practical building blocks in parent-teen communication.

Teens Want to Share

Realize that though, in their hearts, your teens may want to come to you, they may not know how to. You may have a great impact on their lives, but they just can't tell you about it.

For example, do your children *want* to talk to you about that most difficult subject—sex? Yes!

> Most students, 96.9%, thought sex education should come from parents, but only 55.4% thought their parents agreed.
>
> In actual behavior, respondents rated their parents' reaction toward sexual issues/education as follows:
>
> 1. Avoided discussion (43.1%);
> 2. Gave information but discussions were uncomfortable (21.5%);
> 3. Gave basic information and were comfortable (24.6%).[4]

Even parents who think teens ignore them will influence them on this subject:

> The influence of family variables on the sexual attitudes and knowledge of 65 college students was investigated. Parents were rated highest in terms of influence on sexual opinions, beliefs, and

attitudes, but were rated lower than friends, schools, and books as sources of information.[5]

Why not make the most of your influence by speaking out? Chances are that teens who do not talk to their parents on this subject don't do it because they feel their parents would not have time for them or would not be interested. Maybe teens fear embarrassing them. The embarrassment will not live long, once you establish good communication, and it is much better than letting your child make some mistakes that could influence him the rest of his life.

So take the first step and start talking to your child. Then keep talking. If it takes your teen a while to trust you, give him that time. Keep showing that you care, and you'll develop a better relationship.

Challenge your children to excellence. Encourage them to save themselves for marriage. Tell them that as virgins they can someday be like other teens who have given up their virginity—but the others can never again be like them. I challenge girls who are known as "easy" by saying that I can find them hundreds of guys who would spend the night with them, but I've never found one of these guys who wanted to spend a lifetime.

Tell it to your kids like it is. Safe sex is a lie that keeps health clinics in operation. But condoms fail, the pill fails, and so do all other forms of birth control—except abstinence. If you want your child's respect, you have to tell it like it is and never compromise God's standard or your integrity as you share.

I'm waiting for a teen to sue a school or clinic that has given him a condom—and he has still contracted AIDS and is dying. Schools will think twice about promoting so-called safe sex once it costs them $50 million per kid.

Build Trust

If your child doesn't come to you, don't fool yourself that he or she has no problems. Every teen—every person—has problems. But your daughter may feel more comfortable seeking a friend's advice. When she does, she may find her answers in your town's alleys. Your son may find them in the backseat of a car or out drinking and driving.

If you're having trouble getting through to your teen, don't start communication by bringing sex up at the breakfast table tomorrow. Start ironing out your problems here, and you'll fail. Leave the tough spots until you've established some basic communication.

Begin with a personal attitude check:

Do I accept my child's past?
Do I give my child total, unconditional acceptance and love?
Does my child know I will love him, even if he goofs up?
Does my child know that goofing up is just another way of doing something, that it is a part of life?
Does my child perceive that I have time for him?

If you answered no to any of the above questions, you have some work to do. To establish an environment of sharing, you'll need to win your child's trust. Review your answers, then think up a plan of common, everyday ways in which you can teach your child that you want a new start. How can you show your child he's forgiven? How can you show your love? How can you prove to him that you want to spend time together?

Your child needs to know that you will treat him lovingly and will have time for him. The only way he *can* know that is if you show him.

Do you have a tough situation with your child? It's never too late to improve it! With God's help, all things are possible. Spend time with Him and seek new directions for your relationship. Then make yourself available to your teen.

Express Interest

Perhaps you *have* provided the basic support your teen needs, but you still feel room for improvement; or maybe you've begun to communicate. Now ask yourself the following questions:

Am I hugging my teen regularly?
Do we talk openly?
When my teen is quiet, do I ask, "What's the matter?"
Am I patient when he is extra quiet or moody?

Do I continually encourage my child to talk to me about anything and everything?

At first, when you ask questions, you may feel as if you're prying into your child's affairs, if communication has not been the best. But unless you express concern, you'll never talk with your child about the good and bad things in *both* your lives. Share some of your own worries. Tell about your fears and the things you goofed up when you were your daughter's age. Don't barge into her life, but open yourself, and you will find the sharing beginning.

As your daughter feels free to share, remember to do these things:

Listen: Before you give her any advice, walk in her shoes for a while. Know what you're going to give advice on before you do it. Get the facts. Picture her hurts, pains, and pressures in your mind.

Ask questions. Before you hand out solutions, make certain you have understood your teen's problem and emotions concerning it.

Make gentle recommendations. If your teen needs to turn a situation around, don't order her to do so. You may have more impact if you say, "Have you considered doing this . . . ?" Then leave the final decision up to her. You don't appreciate it if your spouse tries to tell you what to do. So be sensitive to the same decision-making need in your daughter's life.

Do your teens feel that they can't confide in you because you'll beat them down with verbal abuse or the unspoken threat, "I'm going to ignore you because you embarrassed me"? Such methods, aimed at keeping a child in line, fail abysmally. In fact they only widen the gap between parent and teen. As long as you cannot open yourself to your child, share with him, and take on the role of teacher, not dictator, you will not be able to lead him.

I don't want that kind of relationship with my children, so now, while they're young, I'm answering their questions—even the embarrassing ones. If I can tell them now what a swear word or rude gesture means, if I talk to them and give them information suited to their understanding,

I may be able to talk to them when they're fourteen, fifteen, sixteen, or seventeen. By that time, I won't be cool to them, but they may trust me because of the years we've spent sharing.

Don't Forget Discipline

I'm not trying to say that while you communicate you should forget about discipline. Just as a young child who's been warned, "Don't do that again, you'll hurt your sister," and defiantly hits his sister again needs to be spanked, teens need to be disciplined. Youngsters and teens need to learn right from wrong. If a child never sees consequences at home, why should he respect his future boss—or the police?

If you don't teach your child the difference between right and wrong, someone else will give them lessons in it. You probably won't like that. When other teens teach, "Drugs are right. What's wrong with them, as long as you don't get addicted?" or, "So you steal something from the store. They have lots of money there; they'll never miss it" you'll want your child to be able to stand firm. Don't leave important lessons like this to others. As parents our basic choice is this: *Prepare* our kids now or *repair* them later.

Recently I spoke to a mother who cried as she shared the results of someone else's lessons to her daughter. She and her husband had been the last to hear that their daughter had received an abortion at a local clinic. After less than an hour's counseling, their seventeen-year-old daughter made one of the most important choices in her life—and she made a decision that did not reflect this family's faith.

Expect and Inspect

How can you show your child that you really care what she does? One way is to follow up on her chores. You won't show you care if you throw out the order, "Weed the vegetable garden," at her as you dart out the door. You may come home to the same number of weeds.

Consistent caring expects and inspects. Make certain you don't toss an order at her. Tell her exactly what you expect. Let her know it doesn't mean just pulling the two biggest weeds, but doing the whole garden. Show her how you expect it to be done. Then when you come home, inspect the job. Show her how she can improve if it still needs work, and let her try again.

Too many parents find it too easy to tell their child what to do and then leave. When the unweeded garden is still around a week later, Mom becomes irate.

Set a Good Example

Identify areas in which you say one thing but do the other. Do you teach your child to forgive others, but hold a mistake over his head? When Dad is inconsistent, blows his stack for no reason, and punishes his son severely, it leaves a mark on that teen's heart and mind. Dad may try to make up for it and think his son should immediately forgive and forget it. Often that teen will, because it's natural for him to move on.

But the next time the son breaks a curfew, messes up the car, or lies, that teen has to run for President of the United States to regain Dad's trust. What Dad expects he doesn't give in return.

Expecting forgiveness that easily but never extending it until your child has paid creates a poor impression of what forgiveness means. Don't leave your child with that negative emotional and spiritual legacy. Let mistakes blow over!

Or maybe you encourage your child to read her Bible but don't seem to get anywhere. Do you read your Bible in front of her? Has she *ever* seen you read the Bible, outside of church? Do you live out the words you read?

How often do teens hear their parents yelling all the way to church? They argue until the car enters the parking lot, when they become all smiles. Mom and Dad walk into church, greeting everyone happily. But as soon as they get back into that car, they pick up where they left off.

Every child knows that this is hypocrisy.

Or how often do kids hear the order, "Don't yell," from parents who *are* yelling? Of course, I've never done that to *my* three small children (do you believe that?), but I know of parents who have!

When I get tired and stressed out, I often do the things that I'm trying to teach my kids not to do. That's why it's so important to keep spending time with your kids; I call it the regrouping process. When you've made a mistake, bring that bond back together; ask for forgiveness. Many times you won't be able to do this five or ten minutes after you've yelled. Your children may need to be alone for a while. But when they come in contact with you again, give them hugs, hold them, and say, "I'm sorry, will you forgive Daddy?" I tell them how I was wrong and how much I need their help to be the best dad in the entire world. Often that's all it takes.

If this system hasn't been part of your family, make it one. It may take a while for your teens to become used to the change, but I can guarantee they'll like it.

What kind of outlook on life do you show your child? It's easy to tell him, "Have a good, positive attitude," but if you don't model that, your words are in vain. To develop and keep a positive attitude, focus on your blessings. On days when it's trying to be a dad, I often forget how hard I prayed for my children and how thankful I was when I finally received them. Add to this the blessing that none of them is blind, has AIDS or a brain tumor, is paralyzed, or has any other major health problem.

When my kids wake me up too early, I need to focus on those truths. When I've had a hard day, and I come home to a fight, I need to remember that it's all a matter of attitude.

In the survey, teens frequently mentioned that their parents gossip. They see when parents talk behind the backs of others. If Mom gets mad because her daughter has been tattling or her son has spread rumors, maybe she needs to take a look at her own habits.

Turn around your gossip problem by saying positive words about someone. When was the last time you told your teen, "Listen to what I heard about Mrs. MacCready. She's the most wonderful person. She's taken in a disabled boy, whom they said would never talk, and now he's making sentences!" That's the kind of encouragement that spreads, so give it to your child.

Maybe you don't have a problem with gossip or yelling, but you've given your child many prejudices. Don't tell your teen to accept all kinds of people and then object when a person of another race comes to your church. Don't look down on someone who has less money and expect your teen not to follow that, too. How many other little prejudices do we have that we pass on to our children?

How are you at passing on love to your teens? Do they know what it is because they've seen it in your home, or do they only know what the

TV shows? If you don't want love and sex to become synonymous in your child's mind, show her that true love means caring for the other person. It means sharing and being a servant. It means you want to see the person you love fulfilled in his or her own eyes and in God's eyes.

Love has nothing to do with taking or getting what we want. But unless you demonstrate that in your home, your teens are likely to miss the message.

Remember these four words: We cannot *not* model. Our teens watch us all the time, and we are their greatest teachers. We become their number-one source on how to handle life and follow through on commitments.

I'm not trying to say that parents have to be perfect—none of us are. But as we strive to live lives of integrity, as we show them what it's like to struggle and win, we provide our children with important lessons.

The Teens' Responsibility

Not only can't parents raise their children perfectly, children have a lot of input into this relationship. When I asked teens about the ways they could meet parents halfway and communicate more effectively, many didn't answer, but the ones who did gave me some interesting answers:

Talk more
Listen more
Get good grades
Try to understand parents
Don't use drugs or alcohol
Do more chores
Try harder
Be honest
Spend more time with parents
Obey parents better
Take parents' advice

These children know they need to meet their parents halfway. They know they need to earn Mom and Dad's respect, so many answers focused on actions that would gain approval.

Other responses related strongly to communication. Teens know they should learn communication skills and practice them in their families. But when you're young, you usually have limited resources in that area.

Teens badly want supportive communication, but they may not get it. Quite often I hear, "If I really talked to my parents, I don't think they'd like me for what I'd say." These young people fear that they will not receive total, unconditional acceptance and love from Mom and Dad. Perhaps they're the same ones who couldn't answer this question on my survey.

Even when they know the answers, why don't teens do the things they know would bring them closer to Mom and Dad? Maybe past experiences have discouraged them. Dad comes home, after he's been away eight to twelve hours, and he's too frazzled to tune in to his family. His son doesn't want to bother him, or he knows that if he does, Dad will just blow up at him anyway.

Family life takes a lot of effort. If parents aren't willing to make it a priority in their lives, teens won't do it. They simply don't have the knowledge and experience that it takes.

The only way you can communicate with your teen is by both of you setting aside time to be together. You can't have a close relationship if you never spend time with a person. Would you expect to have a close friend whom you never called or visited? No! It's the same within your family.

What perception does your child have of you? If he thinks you don't want to spend time with him, that you'll always judge him harshly, and that you'll always place impossible demands on him, he'll never open his heart to you.

To communicate clearly, you may have to be persistent. It's easier to stay uninvolved, not to ask your child's opinion on something, if you know you'll disagree. But by avoiding the painful subjects, you'll miss teaching and communicating opportunities.

When you have conflicts, remember to treat your child well. If you went to a business and spent some of your hard-earned money, and they took you for granted, didn't treat you with respect, or gave bad service, you wouldn't go back, would you? It's easier to avoid the conflict. But you'll be able to go to another auto-parts store, grocery store, or whatever. You can't avoid the truth that this is your child.

So give your teen the kind of respect you'd want. Confront the issue in love, gently, until you both understand each other's views. Even if you never come to complete agreement, you'll better understand your child. But more often communication will help you agree and draw to her in love.

Don't leave your child network rich but relationship poor. Many teens have club, sport, peer, church, and camp groups that they can take part in, but they may not develop deep relationships in any of them. The family is the best place to learn to build intimate relationships. Help your teen do that.

Action Plan for Parents

1. What barriers to sharing can you identify in your family? Take an attitude check. Have you been supportive of your child? If so, how? If not, what can you do to improve support?

2. Do you frequently express concern for your child's affairs? What kind of response do you get? Do you have some room for communication improvement? If so, read a book, magazine articles, and newspaper articles on communication. How can you learn to effectively share? Do you need some counseling help to break down barriers? If so, seek it through your church or community organizations.

3. Make a date with your child. Go out and talk about anything. Walk on the beach, ride your bikes in the neighborhood, or go out for dinner. Then tell your child you'd like to do this regularly. Make it a part of both your lives.

4. Sit down with your child and two pieces of paper and pencils. At the top of each paper, write: *What I most admire about you.* Go to different parts of the room and spend ten or fifteen minutes writing positive things about each other.

Come back together and share your lists with each other. What things on the other person's list made you feel good?

For younger children, you can do this by talking it out, instead of writing. You'll be amazed at what it will do for your relationship.

8

HOW WOULD I SOLVE AMERICA'S PROBLEMS?

Teens have a lot of creative power, so I decided to ask what they thought America's greatest problems were and how they would solve them.

Teens Think It's a Different World

First, I asked the teens what pressures they faced that their parents never had. One of the things that became obvious is that parents have missed out on sharing some very important struggles with their young people. The list I got from teens was:

Drugs and alcohol
Sex
AIDS
Peer pressure
School/grades

I'm not suggesting that you share all the gory details of your biggest mistakes when you were a teen, but it doesn't hurt to let a teen know you faced peer pressure to do drugs and said no or that you goofed up and have scars to show for it today. It can only help a teen to know that you had tough times making grades. Once your son knows that, you may be able to advise him on the basis of what you did right—or wrong.

But maybe teens aren't so far off in some ways, too. The pressures they face are often more intense than those many of their parents confronted. After all, one of the earliest "All in the Family" shows almost did not make it to air time because it included a scene in which someone was going to change a baby's diaper. Compare that to what you can see on TV today—X- and R-rated movies. Be aware of what runs on cable TV— though I wouldn't recommend your watching such shows.

Another way in which teens were definitely right is that their parents never faced AIDS. Who knows what this 100 percent deadly disease will do in years to come? Because it can lie dormant in the body for many years, only when our teens reach their twenties will many of them begin to suffer from its effects.

One area that did not make it to that list is divorce. Sure, when I was a teen, some parents were divorced, but it was nowhere near today's 50 percent rate. About half of our teens grow up in split homes, but very few of their parents have faced the grief, depression, and insecurity that a teen experiences when Mom and Dad decide they can't keep a lifelong commitment.

Not only that, there's the skyrocketing level of abuse in homes. Physical, emotional, or sexual abuse will scar a child for life, and to whom can she turn for help?

Our teens are overburdened emotionally and mentally. They've seen things we wouldn't even have imagined when we were young. They've been desensitized to so much.

I'm not trying to paint a black picture for parents. Now is not the time for Mom and Dad to give up, but to take part. Become aware of your teen's problems. Become part of her school life, through meetings with teachers, talking about her experiences with her, and keeping up on the latest educational issues.

When you see things that will desensitize your child, don't ignore them. Sure, she may not be able to avoid profanity, cheating, or stealing in school, but you can become aware of the temptations and support her in the situations. Open your home to her friends, but make it clear that while they're there, the language will be clean. That may be a new experience for some youngsters.

Don't sell her short, either. If she sets an example of good language, others may begin to notice—and even stop saying profanity around her. People can be strangely reluctant to offend your daughter if they know she has high standards.

Solutions for a Better World

What did teens identify as some of America's greatest problems? Here are their greatest concerns:

Drugs
Alcohol
AIDS
Sex
War/Iraq
Teen pregnancy
Abortion

Drugs and Alcohol

Maybe the answer *drugs* came easily to teens because they hear so much about them on the news, in the papers, and from friends. Many linked drugs and alcohol together, and I'm glad they did, because it means they know that alcohol is an addictive drug. Unlike many parents, these teens did not seek to hide from the impact alcohol has on lives.

What solutions did they find for this problem? Some of these are surprisingly conservative for the liberal world in which teens live! I'm glad to see that they *are* concerned about these serious threats to their safety. Young people don't just shrug them off or attempt to treat them lightly.

Stricter Laws and Punishments. Our kids recognize that the courts and police have got to work together. When a drug kingpin comes before the courts after having illegally gained $100 million through illegal drug sales, our teens can see that asking him to pay back $60 million to the court system and giving him only six months in jail is not a just punishment.

The Death Penalty.   Unlike many adults, teens see the way these crimes harm our community. For many young people, those who are most hurt by drugs are friends, family, and schoolmates. They have a natural urge to fight these crimes in the proportion to which they see the hurt drugs cause.

Teach More Refusal Skills.   It's easy to tell a kid, "Just say no." But even young children need to know how to say, "Never."

Teens need people and self-esteem skills and character in order to say no. It's not enough to say no once; they have to be able to say it over and over again, and that takes a lot of strength. When others put them down for being afraid, a goody-two-shoes, and so on, they need to know that sometimes you simply do things because they are right. No matter what the pressure, they need to stand firm. Here is yet another area in which your life-style, day in and day out, models for your kids how responsible, character-filled people say no to wrong things and yes to right things.

More Cops on Duty.   Young people have asked me, "Why don't the police wipe out drunk drivers by going to bars at night and catching the people who stagger out to their cars, get in, and drive away?" That's a good question. Maybe it's because the police don't receive the community and legal support that would make it worthwhile. But when you compare that cost to the thousands of lives that would be saved, can you really make a case for ignoring drunk drivers? What is your community doing to keep drunks off the road? How can you help?

Stop Dealers.   Young people know who the dealers in our communities are. They learn which adults open their homes to booze parties, which kids sell drugs on the bus, and the other details of the drug trade. In my opinion, we've never solicited the help of the young people who want to see such crimes stopped. By doing this, we encourage them to go along with the wrong.

Check Planes Coming Into the United States.   Massive efforts have been made to stop drugs from coming in, but they never seem to be enough. How could we stop the drugs from coming in when, according to what I've heard, the number-one place for drugs in America is our prisons? These places with bars and gates around them, surrounded by armed guards, have drugs. No armed effort will totally wipe out drug use.

Only when the market for drugs dries up will the drug trade end. So we have to reach the people—the teens—who use the drugs with good reason to say no and the skills to do so.

Only Sell Alcohol in Bars.   Our society tries to sell alcohol to teens by condoning alcohol advertising that aims at young people, so how can we have any control over it? How many of us even desire to keep alcohol sales strictly limited? What are we doing about it?

Counseling for Criminals.   Many of the people who commit drug crimes are living in pain. If counseling could reach them and turn them away from the drugs, we would scale down the drug war. Few drug dealers receive the kind of support and counseling that can turn a life around. Though America may talk a good game, how many people make an effort to visit prisoners and give them hope or to take part in their rehabilitation after they leave jail? How many churches have jail ministries or encourage ex-cons to learn a new way of life in their congregations?

Speakers to Educate Teens on the Subject.   When I spend an hour and a half in a school assembly, only fifteen minutes of that time deals specifically with drugs. Teens need to learn a more basic lesson—that drugs are worth saying no to. They have been taught all about the specific drugs, but they have not learned that they are special people— that saying no is important because they have abilities that they must be sober to use. Only by making the most of their abilities can something great come out of their lives. When teens think no one cares about them and they have nothing to offer, it's easy to "just say yes."

More Nonalcoholic Activities for Young People.   Teens want to be part of a crowd, but when the crowd they know drinks, it seems they must go along with them or have no friends. That's a hard decision to make. Parents can help by making sure teens have more drug- and alcohol-free activities. Don't just plan one big, lock-in, all-night party in May, before graduation. Make a week-in, week-out effort to have something going on. Let teens know what the expectations are for their behavior—and enforce them!

In addition, families need to spend time playing games, sharing, and going places together.

Much Greater Parent Involvement. Our young people realize they cannot fight drugs alone. They need help from Mom and Dad.

Make Alcohol Illegal. I wish this could happen, but I doubt it will. I know firsthand the pain alcohol can cause, and it makes me support such an idea. But the alcohol companies have so much money behind them, and Americans support their "right" to drink strongly enough that I doubt it will happen.

More Narcotics Anonymous and Alcoholics Anonymous Programs. Teens—especially those who experience it in their own families—see the benefits of having planned and prepared, step-by-step programs for people to lean on. They know how much help a recovering addict needs, and they want their parents to seek help.

Turn to God. This answer came way down on the list, but at least some teens realize that it is important. I can testify that this is true, because if God had not come into my life, today I would be an alcoholic. If not for Him, I probably would have been killed. Certainly I would not be doing my work today, with and for teens, if not for the change He brought to my life.

AIDS

Even though many teens do not yet know someone with AIDS, they see the importance of it. When I ask in my assemblies how many teens know someone with AIDS, maybe one in a hundred hands goes up. Only 4.2 percent of the students I surveyed knew someone with the disease. But by 1994, experts predict that one out of every three hands will go up. They say AIDS is like a snowball—one that's rolling downhill fast.

In such a situation, how can we encourage our teens to use "safe sex"? Hasn't anyone ever told the teachers of the liberal sex-ed programs that premarital sex isn't safe? The government tried to warn young people when it published a letter that said:

> Young people must be told the truth—that the best way to avoid AIDS is to refrain from sexual activity until as adults they are ready to establish a mutually faithful monogamous relationship.
>
> But an AIDS education that accepts children's sexual activity as inevitable and focuses only on "safe sex" will be at best ineffectual, at worst itself a cause of serious harm.[1]

When we tell teens less than that, we don't tell them the truth—and we encourage them to include something that's second-best, or even deadly, in their lives.

Does your school simply accept that teens will have sex and only barely mention abstinence? Does it hand out condoms, passing on the message that you have to have sex to be cool? Believe it or not, that's *not* the message our teens want to hear! Here are the suggestions—some of them surprisingly radical—they gave for stopping AIDS:

Abstain from premarital sex and extramarital sex

Separate gays

Teen AIDS testing

Teach the laws of the Bible

More honesty

Better protection for sex

Have laws against having sex with someone when you know you have AIDS

Save sex for marriage . . . and marry a virgin

Get rid of drugs completely so people are not using dirty needles

Put all the AIDS victims on an isolated island

Get rid of the gay communities

Teach kids more about AIDS and how you get it

I'm not seriously suggesting that we make use of all these ideas, but they do show us two things:

Teens know the answers concerning how they can avoid AIDS

Teens are afraid of AIDS and take it seriously

It's not that our teens need more information about the disease, but they do need skills in avoiding bad situations, saying no, and making good decisions.

Premarital Sex

I feel that the teens who answered my questionnaire were very open and honest with me, and they told me that premarital sex is the third problem our country faces. Their concern for it came before war, education, and crime.

Deep down, most teens know that premarital sex is wrong, even if they haven't had much teaching on the subject. They know what they should do, but have trouble carrying out that knowledge. They suggested:

Learn to say NO
Save yourself for your husband/wife
Don't give in to peer pressure
Teach kids the harmful results of sex before marriage
Teach morals
Stand for what you believe is right
Parents should be a good example
Follow the laws of the Bible
Say no to all sex
Don't watch the junk on TV that teaches no values

Parents need to become more aware of the kind of encouragement, teaching, and reinforcement that will help teens say no.

War

When I asked teens about our greatest problems, we were building up to the Persian Gulf War. Though they have a sharp awareness of their own problems, teens also know about and fear what goes on in our world. They can see the dangers of war.

One day our teens will be running this world. I'm glad to know we have some who care about our nation and our world, who want to make them better places.

Pregnancy and Abortion

Number six on the list was teen pregnancy. Young people recognized it as a problem, which isn't surprising, since an out-of-wedlock pregnancy can so strongly impact their lives. Their suggestions for this were:

Abstain until marriage
Have safe sex
Teach kids the facts about sex and pregnancy
Learn to say no
Use some kind of protection
Stick with your values and don't have sex

Seventh on their list was abortion—and it was always on the list. Teens recognize that abortion is murder.

Today America has become a battleground over this issue. Our young people feel pressure from both sides, and they don't know where to turn.

Of course the same solutions teens recommended for pregnancy would help avoid abortions. But how many of our teens recognize that even the "best" birth-control methods fail? Since answer number two on avoiding pregnancy was "have safe sex," obviously many teens do not want to give up sex and have the idea that premarital sex is, at worst, a calculated risk. They have little idea that their lives could be affected by a pregnancy, even though they used "protection."

Since the school system may not tell teens the whole truth, it's up to parents to make the facts available to them. Show your teen the value of abstinence, the fallacies of "safe sex," and the spiritual benefits that come with self-control.

Action Plan for Parents

1. How *does* your teen's world differ from the one you grew up in? How is it the same? Share with your teen some of the differences and similarities you see. How does your teen view them? Do differences mean that you cannot help your teen make wise decisions? Why or why not?

2. Talk to your teen about the pressures you faced while you were her age. Do you think you handled them well? What did you do right? What did you learn from your mistakes?

3. Has your teen handled some pressure well? Poorly? What did he learn from the situation? How could he have done better?

4. Discuss ways you and your teen can make your house a good place for her friends to visit. What do they like to do? What are the house rules? Think of ways you can encourage your child's friends and make them feel at home.

5. How does your teen feel when he has to say no to a temptation? What helps him say no and stay strong? Discuss how he can avoid some temptations and keep from getting trapped by others. Identify moral truths, character qualities, and people skills that will help him say, "Never," at the right time.

6. What does your teen see as one of America's greatest problems? Why does it concern her? Check out what your community or state is doing on these issues. How can you help? Together work on an action plan that can become part of your family life, school, or community project.

9

WHY DO I SOMETIMES MAKE POOR DECISIONS?

If teens have so many people to look up to and good input, and if they know what the big problems are, why do they still make so many decisions to drink, use drugs, and have premarital sex?

To discover the answers to this thorny question, I asked the teens themselves.

What Drugs Are Most Used?

First, I asked about the drugs teens used the most. Alcohol was rated number one, wherever I went. Since I requested the three most-used drugs, marijuana and cigarettes also had high ratings. Depending on the location of the school, answers also included:

Speed	LSD
Crack	Hash
Cocaine	Penicillin
Chewing tobacco	Aspirin
Steroids	PCP
Snuff	Skunk weed

You name it, and I heard it.

Though the beer companies may not want to admit it, our teens know what the greatest addictive drug is in their own school system. They see it every day. Still the companies that sell this stuff try to claim that advertising will not cause young people to drink. When I took an advertising degree in college, I learned how companies advertise to achieve their goal of making people want to buy products. Beer companies are no different from other businesses.

The people who want to sell your children beer do not stop to worry about the traffic accidents, deaths, family problems, and crimes this product causes. Perhaps they are living in a dream world of beliefs that say, "Everyone who buys this can handle it. As long as they only have one or two drinks, it will be okay." But the statistics prove that that's often *not* what happens. Teens drink, drive, and have accidents. People die.

Advertising doesn't focus on those truths. Instead it portrays drinkers as successful, happy, beautiful, and attractive to the opposite sex. Teens need to know the truth, but if you don't tell them, who will? Must they die—or must they lose some of their best friends?

Marijuana, the second drug on our list, has been argued over for years. Groups like NORML (National Organization for the Reform of Marijuana Laws) want to legalize this drug and oppose our country's efforts to fight drugs. NORML looks upon marijuana as a "harmless" drug, ignoring the fact that it is a "gateway" drug that can lead to harder, even more damaging drugs. The majority of people who have used cocaine, crack, and other life-threatening substances started with alcohol, marijuana, or tobacco.

In case you think drug-advocacy groups are harmless, realize that the move to legalize drugs "is moving into the mainstream and becoming increasingly legitimate." According to a one-time NORML attorney, " 'We've made opposition to the government's drug war respectable. . . . We see the drug war as making for a more dangerous society.' "[1]

Want some good reasons *not* to go along with drug legalization? Read through these "Concise Arguments Against Legalization of Drugs," by Joan Bell and Connie Moulton:

The first and foremost reason for not legalizing drugs is that the U.S. is a signatory to the Single Convention on Narcotic Drugs of 1961 and the Convention on Psychotropic Substances of 1971 which obligates us to establish and maintain effective controls on substances covered by treaties. The credibility of our country throughout the world is at stake.

In a recent ABC poll, 90% of Americans disagreed with the idea of legalizing drugs.

Surveyed high school students stated that the illegality of drugs is a deterrent to use.

Our present system of drug regulation and control through licensed handlers still results in over 20 million Americans using prescription drugs for non-medical reasons. We need more stringent controls over the prescription writers.

Adults' use of drugs in the home results in substantially increased use by their children.

Legalization will decrease the number of drug arrests and increase the number of arrests for violent crimes.

Psychoactive drug use results in violent behavior, influencing users to commit crimes that have nothing to do with supporting the cost of their drug habit.

Child abuse cases and the number of drug-addicted babies would increase.

After Great Britain legalized heroin, the addict population increased, the Black Market remained active, and the majority of legal addicts continued criminal activities.

The Dutch took a liberal attitude toward drug use years ago, and today Amsterdam is one of Europe's street crime capitals and a haven for addicts.

A Stanford University study of commercial pilots demonstrated that 24 hours after smoking one joint, the pilots could not land a plane safely. They were shocked. They *thought* they were free of the drug's effects.

The hidden message of legalization is that it's okay to use.

Legalizing drugs will not diminish drug-related profits. It may shift them, but the Black Market would still exist.

Alcohol-related illnesses declined dramatically during Prohibition, then soared after repeal. Greater availability of the substance results in greater use.

Is the discussion turning from the health and welfare of the American people to economics and enforcement?

Will the FDA follow current guidelines for pre-clinical and clinical studies to give approval for over the counter drugs?

What about legal action for health problems caused by the sale of drugs?

How will we control drug use in public places?

Would legalization and taxation generate enough funds to pay for the health problems? Does it now with alcohol and tobacco?

Is all of this legalization rhetoric leading back to the old "hard drug/soft drug" philosophy and paving the way for the legalization of marijuana as a "fall back" position? Is all of this a smoke screen to hide the real purpose—the legalization of marijuana?

We are all affected—especially those who share the roads with drug-impaired drivers.

The lessons of history are clear: the social acceptance of dependence-producing drugs appears to increase rather than decrease all of the problems associated with drug addiction.

Used by permission of Connie Moulton.

Why Do Teens Drink?

When I asked teens, "Do you drink alcohol?" I received some confusing responses: 36.6 percent said yes, and 55.5 percent said no; but when I spoke to some teens, they told me that right now they were not drinking, though they had in the past and intended to do so in the future—and they had answered *no* to my question. Perhaps I should have stated it differently, and my statistics here may be a bit low. According to another source, "In a 1987–88 survey of over 200,000 junior and senior high-school students by the National Parents' Resource Institute for Drug Education, (PRIDE), over 45 percent said they drank liquor."[2]

I asked teens for three reasons why they drank, but I believe that many of their answers could apply to drugs, too, since alcohol *is* a drug. Over 59 percent answered that they drank "to be cool" or "to fit in."

Another 17 percent answered they did it because of peer pressure. I think the first two are also largely the result of peer pressure.

In my survey, over 50 percent of the teens said their parents drank. I'd like to suggest that this, too, is a reason for teen use of alcohol. When young people see Mom and Dad drink week in and week out, they get to thinking that drinking is safe. After all, they haven't seen their parents have any of the harshest side effects that they've heard about, so teens begin to think it's okay. Mom and Dad use this as a way to enjoy life and celebrate. If parents seem to need alcohol to be happy, the children are likely to need it, too.

Why else did teens drink? Here are some of the other findings of my survey:

Bored
To relax
For the taste
To feel older
Curiosity
Because parents do
Because of depression
Because of a challenge
Because they are stupid
For attention
To be rebellious
For something to brag about
Addiction
Because of loneliness
School
Excuse to have sex
To show emotions
Because it is available
To get a boyfriend or girlfriend

Not only are these findings disturbing, today's level of drinking is worse than I believe it was in my generation. When I was in high school, I, too, drank to go along with the crowd, but seldom did we drink to get drunk. According to the students I surveyed, 21.8 percent drank to be drunk, a finding backed up by the PRIDE survey, which said, "A third of the drinkers said they 'got bombed' when they drank."[3]

Before parents give up on their drinking teens, though, they should consider this: "A national survey on drugs and drinking asked teens in 1987 to name the most important antidrug action parents can take, 44 percent said parents should talk with kids about their problems."[4] Caring parents *can* influence their teens to turn around. They can help them say no to the bad things and yes to the good.

I don't believe most teens really want to turn to drinking. Many of them had a fairly conservative approach to booze parties; nearly 50 percent in each school—and sometimes as many as 80 percent—replied that the police should raid them.

As we've already seen, this is an idea that few teens have learned from their parents. When I ask parents, "How many of you have called the police, told them who you were, and had them raid a teenage booze party?" I receive a heavily negative response. In fact, in the last five years I've had less than ten people raise their hands, in all my audiences combined.

This kind of attitude filters down from the top. We can't pass it on to our teens when we're unwilling to take action. Nor can we expect our police to confront the issue, when we don't respect them, back them up, and give them a chance to enforce the law. Perhaps we need to challenge them by telling them we expect them to arrest those who drive drunk and any teens who drink alcohol—period. As long as we unreasonably fear police brutality more than we want to enforce the law, we will suffer the consequences.

Why Do Teens Have Sex?

The number-one answer to this question was peer pressure, but there were a multitude of other interesting responses, some obviously expressed by disapproving teens.

Enjoyment	Emotions
Popularity/to fit in	Loneliness
To be cool	Wanted to get pregnant
Curiosity	To prove a point

To experience something new	Don't want to be a virgin
To feel loved	No morals
Because I'm in love	Rebellious
Desire	R- and X-rated TV
To feel grown up	To get respect
To keep a boyfriend/girlfriend	Looking for happiness
To brag	Marriage
We were drunk	Depression
To make others feel good	Bored
To use someone	Release pressure
To get attention	Because I think it's safe
Don't care about themselves	

How many of those ideas listed had to do with fitting in with the crowd, alleviating emotional pain, or getting back at someone? How many teens realize that having sex outside marriage only leads to pain? The number-one area in which I counsel teens that has caused them to feel hurt and betrayed is when their lover has left them. Outside marriage, sex is neither emotionally nor physically safe.

Can teens say no to sex? Yes! "95% of *Swedish girls* have participated in sexual relations before their 20th birthday. About 66% of *American girls* have experienced sex by that age, but only 17% of unmarried *Japanese girls* have lost their virginity before 20."[5] It's not unrealistic to expect teens not to have sex, but that won't happen if you hand out condoms in schools.

Help your teens to avoid premarital sex by following these simple guidelines.

Bring the Subject Up When They Do. Don't force sex into every conversation. Let the questions that come up in life bring natural moments for explanation. Give a child what he or she needs at the time, instead of overwhelming your youngsters by giving too much too soon.

Don't be like the mother of a little boy who asked, "What is sex?"

Nervously the mother started to explain the best she could, but didn't seem to get much response. As she began repeating herself, she asked, "Why do you need to know?"

"I'm sorry I bothered you," replied the bewildered boy. "I just wanted to know which square to put the X in, beside my name, where it said 'Sex.' "

Don't Be Afraid to Explain. If your child has a question about profanity, which may have been used at school or been written on a wall, use it for a good purpose. Explain God's purpose for sex. Tell how people have perverted that purpose and made sex into an everyday thing.

Give Them the Emotional Facts. Quite often I've heard of teens who wanted to have sex to keep a boyfriend or girlfriend or to feel loved. That's part of the peer pressure that leads teens into a poor decision.

Give your teens the emotional facts. Let your daughter know that the moment she has sex with a boy, in his eyes, she is used, conquered, and no longer a challenge. Usually the boy will be history in her life, and she will feel hurt. In the long run, emotionally she will suffer more by giving sex outside of marriage.

Help Your Teens Avoid Bad Memories. Often teens say they want to experience sex to be cool or feel good about themselves. Tell them that feeling good about themselves will be hard when they cannot forget the sexual experiences they have had outside marriage. If your son has had seven sexual experiences before he marries, his wife will probably not live up to all seven lovers. What woman would want to live up to those seven memories?

When your son breaks up with someone, he will probably never date her again, but he has taken something precious from her. That loss will make her feel terrible and used.

Help Your Teen Look to the Future. Before your son goes out on a date, share this story with him.

"Do you plan on marrying this girl you are dating tonight?" a father asked his son.

"No."

"Will you treat her with respect and honor?"

"Oh, of course."

"Do you plan on getting married sometime?"

"Yes."

"How old do you think your wife is, even though you haven't met her yet?" the father went on.

"Probably seventeen, like me."

"What do you think she's doing tonight?"

"Probably going on a date somewhere with some guy."

"How do you hope that guy treats her? Do you want him to give her respect?"

All of a sudden the teen became very serious. "If he touches her, I'll kill him!"

"Please remember, tonight you are dating someone else's future wife. Treat her the way you'd want him to treat *your* future wife," his father advised.

Help Your Teen Really Prepare for Marriage.   Many teens are curious about sex, and they have sex the first time because they crave the experience. Since they have fallen for the popular myth that you need to have that experience in order to be a good sex partner and they want happy marriages, they may even think they're doing something right. But the fact of the matter is that experience is a hindrance, not a help to a good sex life in marriage.

Instead teach your children to have communication skills. Encourage them to learn to talk and get along with others and themselves. If they have experience in people skills such as talking, listening, caring about others and serving them, and having a well-balanced life, they will have what they need for a happy marriage. Married couples can spend their lives learning about sex. Let your teens know it's right to enter marriage innocent in this area.

Alert Your Teen to the Dangers of Social Pressure.   Teens do have sex because of social pressures. "Teenagers say that social pressure is the 'chief reason why many teenagers do not wait to have sexual inter-course until they are older.' "[6] Your children see sex on TV and hear about it in school and the community. When the "whole world" seems to think premarital sex is okay, teens have to have reasons why no is a good answer.

Spend time watching TV with your teen and point out that television uses sex, not to portray reality, but to sell an idea or product. Ask your teen, "If you have sex, how many of those people who pressured you will be there to help you with the emotional pain, the physical hurts, and the memories?" Chances are that "society" will neither know nor care.

Warn Your Teens About Sexually Transmitted Diseases. Though they hear about them, teens may not really believe STDs could happen to them. Share these facts with them:

> About 2.5 million under 20 are infected with some form of sexually transmitted disease, including AIDS.[7]
>
> Any increase in the more than 50 diseases and syndromes classified as a sexually transmitted disease, or STD, is of concern because these conditions, even excluding AIDS, already account for more than 13 million cases and 7,000 deaths annually, according to the United States Public Health Service.[8]
>
> According to the federal Centers for Disease Control (CDC), the nation is in the grip of an STD epidemic that infects an average of 33,000 people a day. . . . At this rate, 1 in 4 Americans between ages 15 and 55 eventually will acquire an STD.[9]

Consider only a few of the fifty diseases your teen could avoid by not having sex now:

> Cervical dysplasia
> Cervical cancer
> Venereal warts
> Gonorrhea
> Syphilis
> AIDS
> Genital herpes[10]

Aren't those some good reasons to put off sex until marriage?

Helping Teens Make Good Decisions

By encouraging your children to have good images of themselves, you can give them stronger resources with which to say no to sex, drugs, and other poor options. If a teen feels loved within his family, he will better be able to say no. If he has a strong faith in God, he will have the moral fiber to do what is right instead of what others want him to do.

As much as possible, build into your teens the strength of character that will make good decision making a life-style.

Action Plan for Parents

1. What drugs are most commonly used in your child's school? Does your son or daughter know the dangers of drugs? Together discuss why teens feel tempted to use them despite the dangers and provide your child with ways to fight back against the temptation.

2. Watch some TV advertising as you share a program with your child. Point out what the advertiser is using to sell the product. Is it sex, "feeling cool," following the crowd, or something else? Compare the image the advertising portrays with reality.

3. How do you feel about legalizing drugs? How does your child feel? Together read and discuss this chapter's list of reasons not to legalize them. Do you agree or disagree with these reasons? How have they made you change your thinking?

4. What does your teen know about the emotional and physical dangers of premarital sex? Talk over with your child the hurts that it can cause and how he or she can avoid them (*see* Appendix II for more guidelines). Give your teen ammunition against peer pressure by providing the facts.

5. What impact does the need to fit in or be popular have on your teen's actions? How do friends influence your child's thinking? Do those friends encourage your teen to do things that are not approved of in your home? How can you help that child resist or avoid such pressures?

10
WHAT'S GOING ON IN SCHOOL?

Teens spend so many hours in school, you might say that they're experts at it, from their own point of view. After all, they are most influenced by what happens there, so I asked them a series of questions on the challenges and problems they face every day.

Motivation, Challenge, and Discipline

When I speak to teens, I keep hearing this message: They would like to have teachers treat them more like people, love and respect them more, challenge them more, and give them tougher discipline.

Motivation

When I asked teens to list the things that would motivate them in school, I received a combination of practical advice on education and a recognition of teens' own social needs and their weakness in social-relation skills. The first four answers were:

Have more activities/dances/drug-free parties
More speakers/assemblies
Better choices of classes
Better teachers

Those that focused on social-relation skills included:

Individual help
People who will listen and talk more
More groups and clubs that I fit into
More rewards and recognition
Compliments
Show respect
Be stricter
Stop verbal abuse

Despite that list of good ideas for improvement, teens did not really feel their schools were complete failures, though.

A Caring Challenge

More than three-quarters of the teens who answered my survey felt their teachers challenged them enough. Young people need to have teachers who care enough about them to challenge them. As long as no one presses them to do their best, like people of any age, teens will fall short of their greatest accomplishments. But at the same time, both parents and teachers need to be certain teens have an outlet. Overwhelming pressure will cause more harm than good. So young people need to be able to talk over pressures, deal with them, or even occasionally avoid them.

According to my survey, 65 percent of the students feel their teachers cared about them personally. Teachers who see their students as people, not just objects, are more likely to treat them well, to understand the pressures of the teen years, and offer help in tough situations. The challenges need to be offered in love, not out of a pure desire to see good statistics.

Discipline

Though they often don't give this impression, deep down, teens want to have rules. They want to know they can't get away with murder in the classroom. They don't want to be able to get away with cheating. But like many other humans, if they can look over their shoulders during a test—and not be punished—they will. Sure, some teens won't cheat, even if they have the opportunity, because they have strong moral values. But in a society that encourages moral freedom, only those who have seen the flaw in a loose moral life-style will withstand the temptation.

Encourage teachers who are giving your teens the kind of challenge they need. Help them do the best job they can by giving them feedback and support.

Parents Who Take Part

When I asked teens if their parents visited the school during the year, over half said yes. In many schools the figure ran from 60 to 70 percent. But often that meant that Mom and Dad only visited once a year.

When I go into a school and seven or eight hundred parents come out to my evening session, I feel encouraged. Often the teens went home and said, "I like this guy. You've got to come tonight. He has a good message for the whole family. Let's go together." Countless parents have told me their teens passed on that message, and I feel encouraged, because I know such parents listen to their teens. They take the risk of coming out and hearing about their problems in public. Though they do not know what I am going to say, they believe in their children enough to come.

But other teens come up to me after an assembly and confide, "I wouldn't dare ask my parents to come tonight. They just don't go to events like this." When I talk about serious hurts in the family, I often hear, "Mom and Dad told me not to tell anyone about this. They say we should just keep it within the family." When alcoholism, abuse, or a parent with an uncontrolled temper has harmed them, a family often institutes a "no talk" rule. They will rarely be open to community contact.

The Need for Involved Parents

The statistics concerning our children and school are encouraging. But we must remember that teens see education from a limited point of view. Naturally few will ask for more homework. They do not have a long-term perspective that parents have on what is in their best interests.

Let's use the survey as a basis for parents to see ways they can become involved in their schools.

What kind of message have Mom and Dad given teens and educators about what goes on in public schools? Have we let teens believe they live in two worlds, by letting the school go off in one direction, while our homes go in another? Have we led educators to believe they can do as they please, without regard to the community opinions? There are solutions, if parents will become involved.

Start with preparing for a fact-finding mission by visiting your child's teacher.

What Do I Say? So you've decided to take part in your child's schooling. You've agreed with yourself to call the teacher. Now what?

Before you make an appointment, take a look at your child. What are her strong points? Her weak points? Where have you seen real growth—or a need for it? What unachieved goals does she have? How could you or that teacher help? Does your child have trouble in a specific subject? Do you have any ideas for solutions?

Then consider the teacher. How can you encourage him? What has he done well in? Do you see some areas for improvement? How could you tactfully express this?

My daughter Emily was very shy in first grade. She had a hard time getting up in front of the class to share and talk. It would have been easy for Holly and I to ask the teacher to excuse Emily from all such activities, and it certainly would have been simpler for the teacher. But we didn't do that. Instead, the three of us lovingly but persistently encouraged Emily to share. Because Holly and I wanted our daughter to grow, we kept in touch with the teacher, who helped Emily greatly in this area. Now that Emily is going into third grade, we can see the results of that team effort.

Remember, do not nag the school when you make such contacts. Use tact when you express the need for change, and make certain you encourage people.

As a Christian parent, in a public school system you are probably going to run into ideas that do not agree with your own. If you cannot tolerate anything that goes against your faith, perhaps you would do better sending your child to a private Christian school. But those parents who are willing to stand up for basic moral principles that teens need to learn may find that they have a strong impact on their school. Just because you're Christians, don't fall for the lie that you cannot confront the school when it teaches things that disagree with Christian morals. Believers need to be willing to stand up in their communities—firmly, lovingly, tactfully, and gently.

Before parents criticize the school system, they should do their homework. If you've noticed a problem, find out what *is* being taught. Visit the school, talk to teachers, and ask about the curriculum. If you receive permission from the principal, you can even go in and observe classes, if necessary. Don't believe all rumors you hear. Investigate for yourself.

The Moral Environment

When I go into schools, I often see that teens take subjects like cheating, lying, stealing, the use of profanity, drugs, and premarital sex very lightly. The attitude seems to be, "It's no big deal. What's the problem?"

According to one study, if you see a heavy drug problem, it may indicate that many families in your community are also in trouble:

> Among young people who have been physically or sexually abused, many turn to drugs. In a recent study of 400 youth in a juvenile detention center in Florida, a team of researchers established a strong correlation between child abuse and later drug use.
>
> The researchers also discovered a clear pattern in the family backgrounds of the youth in detention. "Only 14% of the youths—in the study—lived with both their biological parents," note these criminologists, "and 54% indicated they resided with either their mother only or their mother and other relatives. A majority of the detainees reported they did not live continuously with both their biological parents for their first 12 years."
>
> This new study underscores the difficulty of reducing child abuse or drug use without strengthening family life.[1]

As parents, we cannot ignore our children's needs. We need to provide a strong family background, in which teens are supported, loved, and disciplined. But we need not ignore the threat that can become a part of a school system when teachers ignore Judeo-Christian family values and attack the traditional family.

Remember, your teen is still forming his or her value system. What she hears in school may confuse her, if it conflicts with her upbringing. What others push on him in the classroom may cause him to make some unwise choices. So take part in your child's education by remaining aware of the issues, curricula, and attitudes of those who teach. If good lessons are taught, express your appreciation. If bad ones are taught, become involved in a plan for change.

What Can You Expect Schools to Do?

Educate Consistently. When I asked teens what a school could do to help fight the drug and alcohol problem, they answered, "Educate/teach kids to say no."

Look into the education your teens receive in school. Are they learning, "Don't drink and drive"? If so, realize that they have received a message that indirectly says, "It's okay to drink." This sort of teaching undermines the strong message of morality, ethics, and the law that most parents would like to send their children. Inconsistent messages will undermine a firm morality.

Educators often try to present "value free" ideas. They don't want to offend anyone, so they take the road of least resistance by attempting to teach no values at all. Teachers have learned to do this in their training, and administrators hesitate to deal with opposition from those who object to any morality that is taught—so we have fallen into offering our children either a confusing message or one that totally lacks Judeo-Christian morals.

But don't be fooled. Parents and educators teach morality by example. We simply can't avoid it. We've simply replaced one value system with another. When we attempt "value free" education, we still teach our children moral values: They learn that no one has the courage to say the word *wrong*.

We *must* tell our children the truth: That some things are harmful and will never help you; some things can only damage you. Have you ever met someone who used alcohol as a crutch and ended up better for it?

Have you known of someone who had multiple sexual experiences who became healthier in his sense of self-worth or body? No! Then why leave that door open for our children?

Many school systems have a totally humanistic approach to the human race. They say we were born perfect (though they cannot effectively explain why things are such a mess today). They say we evolved from slime—then how did "chance" make us so "perfect"?

Parents need to make children aware of the fact that they need God's salvation. We are not perfect, but He sent His Son to die for us, to forgive our sins so that we would have a new life. We need to teach the biblical principles that are part of that truth, and we need to encourage our schools to teach them, too.

By leaving your child with a "value free" morality that comes from hours of school training and no parental input, you turn her into a starter, not a stopper. She will experiment with drugs, alcohol, and sex. When no one tells her it is possible to avoid these things—and that she will be happier in the long run if she does say no—she will never discover that God can give her the strength to avoid the things that would hurt her, not help her. She will be confused, because a "values free" message *is* confusing—it contradicts itself.

Parents may feel as if they're barging in on the school system, if they object to what is taught. But large portions of the education system do not want passive parents.

> Blame the Parents! 90% of public school teachers cited lack of parental support as a problem in their schools in a survey of 22,000 teachers in 1988. "Teachers repeatedly made the point that in the push for better schools they cannot do the job alone," Ernest L. Boyer, president of the Carnegie Foundation for the Advancement of Teaching, which conducted the survey, said.[2]

Take educators up on that challenge. Don't be one of those parents who never shows up. Visit school more. Get involved, and you will begin to understand what's going on in our schools and to discover how you can reinforce your values and teachings there.

Provide Support Groups. Over 11 percent of our students wanted support groups, such as SADD, to help. If you call in a support group, be certain you know what you will receive from it. If you encourage teens to drink, but not drive, they *will* drink. The message you've given them allows for it. Likewise, if your support group shows twelve-year-olds how to put a condom on a banana, don't be surprised if the same kids who giggled during this experience go out and use the lesson for its real purpose.

Don't be afraid to challenge teens to do their best. When I talk to young people and challenge them to excellence instead of mediocrity, I receive a standing ovation. When I encourage them to wait to have sex, not just be one of the majority—to be the one who is in demand—they applaud. Real support says, "Right is right and wrong is wrong. Some things are wonderful, but others will not be tolerated, period." Teens know that, deep down.

In one school I spoke in, the staff became angered because I told the students some things were wrong.

"You obviously don't know much about kids, do you?" a coach said to me.

"What do you mean?" I asked.

"We wouldn't have a team if we kicked off all the kids who drank!"

"You are afraid to lose a kid from the team by standing up for what is right," I pointed out. "Because of that you will never gain the teens' respect, and they will never grow in character because you've been in their midst."

Support does not always mean agreement, and teens know it! They want help, not just a pat on the back.

Use Stricter Punishment. Kids understand that certain actions need punishment. As long as we avoid doing this, we give them a double message.

On the campus of the University of Michigan, young people are receiving a mixed message. The university police have been ordered to turn their heads at marijuana use. The police in the city have announced that they will prosecute anyone seen using the drug.

What message does this give young people? That marijuana is legal on campus, but not one step off it? By avoiding the message of right versus wrong, we confuse teens to no end.

Not only did teens want stricter punishments, they also advocated watchdog policies such as keeping a closer eye on students, checking lockers, and giving drug tests. Deep down, teens want parents who are willing to take stands, even those that might not agree with what the rest of the system is doing. To parents, such steps seem too controversial, and they resist doing something that will not go along with their crowd— the adults and administrators who would disapprove. Parents have fallen into the peer-pressure trap they object to in their teens' lives.

Can you accept being a bit controversial, if it means giving your teen a clear message of right?

Offer Good Speakers. Some teens wanted more speakers to talk about drugs. If you decide to have a speaker, check carefully on the message that person will give and the life-style he or she will portray. If you invite a speaker who tells your teens to say no to drugs but who tries to dance with the high-school girls, even though he's married, you are not giving a consistent message.

You also need to be concerned about what teens will hear if they write to a speaker. I know, because I speak in schools, that many teens who do not have a father, big brother, or other authority figure will take the time to write a speaker. A morally sound one may help a teen. But what about the person who does not have good morals? Do you want your teens to receive that message?

My wife, Holly, is on a committee that brings entertainment to our children's elementary school. She checks out the people, finds out about their message, listens to a tape, and then decides what should be done about hiring them. But she keeps in mind that the message must fall in line with the morals most parents want their children to hear.

Provide Counseling. Some teens wanted counseling, but many schools feel reluctant to become involved in this area.

How desperately some teens need help! If the school does not offer it, they may feel they have nowhere else to turn. When the family passes on the message, "Don't tell anyone," a teen feels reluctant to spill the beans. Unless you make it easy for them to tell, you may encourage the coverup.

I'm not advocating untrained teachers acting as counselors. But a school can make contact with the properly educated people in the community, who can help these children and their families. Many teens desperately need answers for serious problems.

Encourage Parental Involvement. Some teens also recognized the need for parental involvement. As long as parents do not work with the schools in areas such as drug use, no one can fight it effectively.

Some principals have told me that when a dad comes into their office with concerns about the curriculum, teacher, or policy, they give that idea more weight. Why? Because most men never come into their school. Few parents get involved at all. The same parents show up for the PTA meetings, policy meetings, curriculum meetings, and so on.

When parents *do* show up at a curriculum meeting, often only three or four want to support the curriculum and shape it in a value-based and morally strong direction. Left to themselves, that may be the direction the school administrators and teachers would take, but when a group that is sympathetic to the gay community appears at the meeting, it may sway the educators to portray the gay life-style as a viable alternative for teens. Though study after study shows that the homosexual population is about 3 or 4 percent of the community, such groups often portray it as 10 percent of the population. They have a reason to encourage young people to move into a homosexual life-style, since that is their only method of reproduction.

Teens also said they needed better curfews—and this is one thing only parents can enforce. Let's face it, parents may establish a curfew, and a teen may occasionally break it; but without a curfew, that child will be more open to making mistakes. A sixteen- or seventeen-year-old does not often have the commitment and character qualities to stick to something his parents do not adhere to.

An article in *Life* magazine described a parent who allowed her daughter to stay out as late as she wanted, as long as she let Mom know where she was. One night the daughter stayed out until 3:00 A.M. Confronted with this, the daughter told her mother that she'd been out with her boyfriend, but she was so shy, they hadn't even kissed.[3]

Maybe that daughter *hasn't* kissed her boyfriend, but if they keep on going out that late, what will happen by their seventeenth date? Shyness will be gone, and kissing will be the least of that mom's problems.

Why don't I let my kindergartners ride their bikes to a friend's house, three miles away? Because they'd have to cross all sorts of busy intersections. Though I've crossed the road with them hundreds of times, and we've ridden our bikes together, and I've showed them how to cross streets with a bike, I know they aren't ready for it. When they are alone, a car honking at them, the road busy, and their minds abstracted, they could be hit by a car. I don't want them to take that chance.

Kids feel more comfortable if we give them rules, because it makes them feel safer. But if we don't give them those guidelines, no one will do it for us.

A Consistent Message

Though we give a message of excellence to the business community, we seldom give our teens more than a message of compromise. Is it any wonder that so many of them have a light moral base to fall back on? No wonder our college campuses run rampant with date rape. Once teens leave high school, they see condoms, packaged right next to the cigarette machines. They live in coed dorms. Can you blame *them* for having a mentality that has become confused?

Where do college kids put their trust? According to a *USA Today* poll:

26% trust TV news;
44% trust educational facilities;
47% trust the U.S. Supreme Court;
21% trust religion;
23% trust major companies.[4]

Compare those statistics to some from a Gallup poll:

In the latest *Gallup Youth Survey*, you will find some interesting information on college students:

About one in four (23%) students polled described themselves as "born again" or "Evangelical" Christians.
Over half (55%) attended a worship service in the last 30 days and about one in four (24%) read the Bible at least weekly.

69% polled did not feel there was anything wrong with premarital sex.

56% approved of trial marriages.

69% believe divorce is acceptable in the case of incompatibility."[5]

More teens are willing to trust in education, the Supreme Court, or big business than in their faith. Granted, I don't trust in "religion," but in Jesus Christ, who has saved me. Yet how can I trust in the TV news more than faith? How can I encourage my child to trust in these things?

Those who claim to be born again face some heavy peer pressure. Look at those high statistics concerning approval of divorce and premarital sex. When over half of our teens attend worship services regularly, how can they come away with such ideas? Can't they see the inconsistency between faith and practices such as these?

Some of this confusion no doubt stems from the fact that what teens hear at home and what they hear at school are different. Caring parents need to limit the amount of confusion that becomes part of their teens' lives by encouraging schools to teach basic moral values that will help teens and not hurt them.

Help your teens to develop consistency. Call home to check on them when they're alone. Encourage them to do better schoolwork; become involved in the parties they are invited to, either by chaperoning them or advising them not to go to dangerous ones. These are all ideas from our teens.

To develop consistency, teens need to see the same message repeated until they know that it is true. Don't tell a teen not to use drugs once and forget about it. Reinforce that over and over, on a daily basis.

Action Plan for Parents

1. Does your teen feel challenged enough at school? Too challenged? Discover why. If you need to make changes, outline the things that cause too great or too little challenge. Then talk to your child's teacher about how you can help.

2. Are the values of your child's teachers Judeo-Christian ones? If not, what are they, and how does this influence your child? How can you encourage that teacher to develop classroom values that will be the best for your child and other students?

3. What sort of speakers come to your school? Do you know what they teach? Can you become more involved in this area of your school system?

4. How have you taken part in your school system? Are you one of the many parents who never contact a school? If so, why? How can you change this?

5. What parent groups are available in your school? Can you become involved in one? Do you need to start one? What would reach parents best and encourage them to become involved?

Part III
WHAT ARE OUR CHILDREN TAUGHT?

Every year I speak in hundreds of schools—most of them public ones. I see teachers who care, who want to see students learn and become the best they can be. I talk to teachers, encourage them, and share the concerns I hear from teens. I speak to caring administrators, too.

Sometimes I also disagree with teachers and administrators. Despite those rare occasions, I keep working in the public-school system. So many teens need the message I have to give them. They need hope, people skills, and self-esteem. They need to know someone cares about them and believes they can live successfully.

No school system is perfect, because no teacher, administrator, or student is perfect. But that does not mean we have to give up. Together we need to work to create a better school, teach students the skills they need, and create a better community.

Some of the ideas you'll find in this section may come as a surprise to you. When I first heard of some of them, I thought the people who told me about them were a bit radical . . . maybe I didn't quite believe them. So I looked into them for myself.

As I did my research, I began to realize that our public-school system can hold some dangers to our children, our society, and our world. Many well-meaning teachers may be influenced by them, and many parents remain unaware of the threat in their own schools.

I'm not trying to tell you that your students receive all the information here or are taught these things. I don't know your school system—the teachers or administrators there. I've never sat in on a sex-ed class or heard what's taught about drugs. But I do want you to be aware of the ideas that some schools have accepted.

Once you become aware of these ideas and how they are used in schools, you can check out your own school system. Learn the facts. Find out how your administrators feel about these ideas and how much latitude teachers have in the classroom. Talk to your child about what is said in class. Compare these ideas to the lesson plan.

As parents we need to be aware of the lessons taught in our schools and the impact they have on our children. To do that, we need to educate ourselves first.

11

WHAT DO WE EXPECT OF OUR SCHOOLS?

We Americans have high expectations for our school systems. Generally we tend to place a high value on them, seeing them as a door to the future—one we want our children to walk through because it will improve their lives.

Even after many years of complaint and confusion about the inadequacies of the public-school system, a report by the National Commission on Excellence in Education, backing itself with a 1982 Gallup Poll, reported that Americans had a strong regard for education. The commission observed three things:

1. Americans considered education more important than developing the best military or industrial systems.
2. They felt it was "extremely important" in insuring their children's futures.
3. They believed it should be the top priority when it came to federal funds.[1]

Despite the changing times, I don't believe parents' desire to see their children well educated has changed. Witness the continuing interest in education and efforts to improve it. Even in the midst of discussions of private-school tax credits, interest in education in public schools remains high. In 1991 the news that SAT scores had again plunged received national attention,[2] as people attempted to identify the problem and its solutions.

Do Americans really care little what is taught in their schools? Are we so apathetic? I don't think so. "A Nation at Risk" found that the public's standards for creating more challenging course offerings went way beyond the strictest requirements in high schools in every state—or even requirements for most college admissions![3]

Why hasn't more change occurred, if we feel this way? Parents may feel the desire to have their children well educated, but they know they are not—by and large—educators themselves. Often they simply leave education in the hands of those who seem to know best.

The Education We Remember

Many parents look back fondly on their school days, remembering how they learned reading (by the phonics method), writing (that demanded correct spelling), and arithmetic (without use of calculators). These core subjects were stressed by all educators—not to teach them would have caused shame to fall on a teacher.

In this atmosphere, education in the basics was something of great value. Teachers and parents agreed that the role of the school was to provide fundamental skills in these areas and instill a love of learning in students. With minimal disputes, parents and teachers worked to prepare children with those things worth learning and necessary for life.

These ideas remain the source of parental respect for and appreciation of schools and teachers. Parents expect that, as in their day, the school system will reinforce parental authority and dignity while it develops a student's academic abilities.

Most parents also expect that the child's personality, values and beliefs are a delicate matter, best left to parents. In the "old days" the inner workings of a child's feelings were clearly off-limits to educators.

But much of today's education no longer follows those patterns. It's not always the way parents remember school. Agendas for educators have changed, and lessons for student teachers have been altered to reflect psychological theories that were unknown to those who taught the three R's. Educators have entered areas that once were off-limits to them—and parents may not even realize it.

In the wake of new attitudes—and massive social changes that have altered the world we remember when we were children—the school system *is* very different. Is it less successful? Do teachers have some real reasons for complaint? Are parents just rabble-rousers who don't know what they're talking about?

It *Is* a Different World

Most parents know that the world has drastically changed. They look at the newspapers and see reports of a high divorce rate, rampant sexually transmitted diseases, and a communications system that they once never would have dreamed of, and they have to admit that their teens don't face the same challenges they did.

Dad goes to a newsstand and sees teens picking up reading he never would have dared bring into the home when he was young. In the library, on open shelves, Mom sees books she wouldn't encourage her teens to read. Television plays shows that debase the family, portray sex as a recreational activity, and offer little hope to hurting teens.

When parents overhear their teens' conversations with friends, those young people may seem part of a different world. How many Moms and Dads aren't aware that teens know more about computers than they do? How many homes have VCRs that only a teen can program?

Some of the changes have provided us with wonderful opportunities—but they have often opened the door to confusion, too. Computers are wonderful methods of communication. But what's being communicated? Teens can learn from videos—but are they always lessons parents want teens to learn?

What Can Parents Do?

In an ever-changing world, can parents compete? Can they find a solid place in the shifting sands around their teens? Yes!

As a child faces this changing world, he needs to have certain ethics, truths, and knowledge that will hold him through the times of stress and indecision. He needs to know what is right and wrong. He needs to have a strong base to work from, and parents can and must provide that.

Look at what happens when teachers face a classroom filled with rowdy students. How much time can be spent on learning math, English, or social studies? If it takes half a period to calm the students, half the information the teacher wanted to communicate may be missed entirely. So parents do have an important role concerning the kind of students who fill our schools. And schools should not undermine that by teaching courses that break down a teen's morality.

Parents also play a critical role in how children view learning, the kind of effort they put into it, and the value they place upon it. When a group of researchers looked into the lives of some exceptional artists, athletes, and scientists, they observed the following common elements in their family lives:

1. The family was hardworking and took part in many activities.
2. Doing one's best was emphasized within the family circle.
3. Parents encouraged children to participate in skill-producing activities.
4. Parents discussed the child's performance, reviewing accomplishments.
5. Parents monitored the child's time and activities.[4]

I'm not saying you have to raise a concert pianist or the next molecular biologist to win the Nobel Prize, but neither do I want parents to believe that education is simply a matter of leaving all the teaching to their school system. Knowing that what you do in the home will influence your child's success is as important as knowing your child has to have a good formal education.

Parents of these high achievers took active parts in their teens' lives. They knew what their children did, gave them input, and supported their efforts. They did not leave youngsters to their own devices or encourage mindless activities. The results of these parents' sacrifice paid big dividends in their children's careers.

I'd like to encourage parents to give their children that kind of attention, but I'd also add that these teens need spiritual nurturing. Because if you only provide a child with career goals, you have not given him a complete understanding of himself or his world. As you nurture a child spiritually, you can also help him develop emotionally and intellectually.

Parents and Teachers

Parents and teachers need each other. Parents usually know that they are not teachers—at least not in the professional sense. Most do not desire to take over the role of teaching their youngsters full time. But Mom and Dad also have a sense of direction for their child that a teacher cannot have.

Teachers need parents, too. Without their support, students will not do homework or behave or pay much attention in class. When students become preoccupied with family troubles, they have much greater trouble achieving well and may actually turn into those having trouble making it.

Teachers who might like to teach well face time constraints, discipline problems, and textbook limitations. Though parents might not have school exactly the way they want it, neither do the teachers.

Only by working together will we correct some of the problems we see in education. Teachers want support. When they get it, they may also receive some conflict from active parents who want to see students achieve. Parents may outline extensive plans for reform, only to be told, "We can't do that, because. . . ."

What I'm advocating is not a short course in mutual harassment. But neither am I encouraging parents to gloss over the sometimes very subtle negative messages that are fed into teens' minds. Teachers do not need parents who only say yes, but they also do not need ones that say no to everything. They need families who will support them, encourage them, and redirect flaws that may cause trouble in education. Parents see their children away from school. If they have an important role in their children's lives, they can see teens from a more natural perspective than most teachers. They can know a child's aspirations, goals, and desires as few teachers—who face classes of thirty students at a time—can. Unless teens are to be lost in the crowd of a school system, they need the parental touch on their education.

Don't create an us-them mentality between you and your school system. Instead, create a communicating, win-win situation for both. Learn how you can work with teachers and teens to create a school that both honors your belief system and educates your child well.

Action Plan for Parents

1. What expectations do you have for your school system? Write out lists of specific goals you'd like to see your child reach this year and by the time he or she graduates. Now look at them from the teacher's point of view. Are they realistic? Do they require your help? Redesign any unrealistic goals.

2. What expectations does your child have for school? Where are potential areas of growth? Can you add them to your plan?

3. How is education different in your child's school from the way it was in yours? What influences have changed education? Have the changes been improvements?

4. What changes would you like to see in your child's education? Once you have developed a plan, contact your child's teacher or guidance counselor to discuss how these can be instituted.

12
A PSYCHOLOGY OF EDUCATION

In school, most parents expect their children to receive cognitive education—the traditional education that focuses on training the intellect. This includes learning academic skills, such as reading, writing, and memorizing the times tables. Parents also expect their children to learn psychomotor skills, such as handwriting, physical education, speech, trade, and technical courses.

However, children may receive something very different from that in the classroom. A school system may have as its goal the one Professor Benjamin Bloom, of the University of Chicago, outlined in his book *All Our Children Learning:* "The purpose of education and the schools is to change the thoughts, feelings and actions of the students."

We've come a long way from the three R's!

Affective Education

The psychology of education that such educators employ is called affective education; in it, how a child feels about himself takes precedence over learning traditional basics. In affective education, small children are forced to make adult decisions about issues such as suicide, murder, divorce, abortion, and adoption.

> Techniques used in the classroom include violent and disturbing books and films; materials dealing with parental conflict, death, drugs, mental illness, despair, and anger; literature that is mostly negative and depressing; requiring the child to engage in the role playing of death, pregnancy, abortion, divorce, hate, anger and suicide; personal attitude surveys and games (such as Magic Circle) which invade the private thoughts of the child and his family; psychological games which force the child to decide who should be killed (such as the survival game); explicit and pornographic instruction in sex acts (legal and illegal, moral and immoral); and a deliberate attempt to make the child reject the values of his parents and his religion.[1]

While parents have thought their children were receiving the basic skills, many have discovered that educators used their teens as guinea pigs for such experimental programs and fads and psychological and behavioral experiments.

Over the last ten or fifteen years, parents have begun to notice the changes and ask questions. They have seen an emphasis on reading and writing change to self-esteem, drug education, death education, AIDS education, and comprehensive school health curricula under a variety of names. Instead of supporting parental values or religious precepts that are learned in the family, affective education focuses on teaching young people to "make their own choices"—choices based on a peer-group consensus.

At home parents have begun to experience a sense of alienation from their children as they have seen them accept ideas that are not a part of traditional morality and our American heritage. Their children seem confused by the conflicting messages they receive.

Nondirective Education

While *affective education* describes the basis for the educational program, *nondirective education* clarifies the type of teacher involvement it will provide. In very clear terms, with this sort of emphasis, which is often associated with affective education, you can expect little or no direction from the teacher.

Nondirective education is based on Carl Rogers's psychological method. In such psychotherapy, instead of playing the role of expert and problem solver, the therapist attempts to avoid giving direction or passing judgment. In teaching, the teacher acts only as a "facilitator," who speaks back to the students, reflecting their own ideas. The student has to arrive at his or her own conclusions and defend them publicly.

Nondirective education is founded on the premise that we live in times of extremely rapid change, and old answers no longer apply to today's problems. Therefore, it claims, we must "set our children free" to come up with their own answers.

People who support nondirective education dangerously assume a child has within him the ability to solve life's problems without any reference to right or wrong and without the benefit of past knowledge.

Nondirective education is not education, because education imparts knowledge. It *is* therapy.

Therapy in the Classroom

Parents who want to identify therapy in the classroom should look for terms such as:

Values clarification
Behavior modification
Moral reasoning
Decision making
Higher-order critical-thinking skills
Humanism
Problem solving

These identify therapy techniques that are commonly integrated into the school curriculum. They will be especially prevalent in courses such as:

Sex education
Death education
Drug education

Family living
Parenting
Citizenship and character education
Global education
Talented and gifted programs

Initially educators brought Rogerian psychology into the classroom in the hope that it would produce increased academic and cognitive skills, along with other forms of scholastic improvement. According to Dr. William Coulson, who worked with Rogers, "But as a matter of fact, in the projects that Dr. Rogers or I had firsthand experience with, it didn't work."[2]

Despite Dr. Coulson's discovery, these educational fads remain in many classrooms. Parents can identify their use in some of the following programs.

Role-playing

Remember when your teen was a young child who imagined characters of all sorts? For a while he may have had a pretend friend, who one day went away. In this sense role-playing is a natural part of a child's development.

Values-clarification experts have seen the worth of taking this idea and turning it into therapy. In this educational technique, teachers encourage children to play certain roles in order to delve into their emotions. They seek self-disclosure from the children in an unnatural fashion. Real feelings that a child often conceals may be brought out by this method, which is also known as sociodrama or dramatic impersonalization.

However such techniques do not only aim at bringing a child's thoughts into the open, they aim at changing them: "Roleplaying is a natural method of learning and unlearning various reactions to complex life problems . . . It seems to have some logical inherent advantages over other methods of psychotherapy since it simultaneously attacks modes of thinking, feeling and behavior—the entire province of psychotherapy."[3]

In the classroom children may experience this when they participate in imaginary roles such as those in the fallout shelter program. During this exercise, children must decide which six out of ten people will live; they face the task of eliminating those who are too sick or unproductive. Another area frequently the focus of role play is reproduction and its purpose.

In role play, children must publicly make value decisions concerning life, death, human worth, moral compromise, and extremely violent death experiences by taking on the role of someone involved in such situations. They are placed in situations that adults struggle with and left there without any direction. The only values that are represented are those the students come up with on their own.

Children might not know better in this situation, but the adults who bring it to the classroom should. What are the possible outcomes of such activities? The innermost feelings of the children are being stalked and preyed upon by adults who full well know that the desired outcome is to invade the private feelings and beliefs of the child and bring about desired personality changes.[4]

Have any of the educators who use role-playing given serious consideration to the facts that this directly violates a child's right to privacy and that parents have not given their permission for such therapy? Role-playing is a form of therapy used by psychiatrists in a clinical setting. What reason does it have for being in the general school system?

Visualization/Hypnosis

Another pair of in-vogue techniques that appear in the school under the guise of stress management are hypnosis and visualization. You may see it in the school under the names basic relaxation techniques, calming response, the quieting reflex, self-regulation, or auto-regulation. Their stated goal is to reduce stress in the child.

Those who encourage students to use this therapy assume that children are under stress and that stress is bad and needs a solution. But as educational analyst Dr. Shirley Correll states:

> We know that one purpose of the conscience is to produce stress. When a person contemplates doing something mean or petty or ugly, the conscience restrains by the use of this stress. Further, we

know that it is the purpose of the conscience either to excuse or to accuse, based upon our values system, and that if the conscience is suppressed often enough, it ceases to function. When a person's conscience is so seared, we call this state a criminal mind.[5]

Values clarification suppresses and may sear a youngster's conscience.

From kindergarten, children are being taught to use relaxation techniques—self-hypnotic suggestion—at the first sign of stress. Though this keeps them in a calm state of mind, it may place them in danger. Rachel Copelan, a certified hypnotherapist, sex educator, and family counselor states, "Not all tension is bad. Some is essential to survival. A certain amount of tension supplies the alertness which is essential for an emergency."[6] Hypnotic techniques have the ability to interfere with what is known as the fight-or-flight response, the body's normal healthy response to a perceived threat.

What is the goal of educators who place our children in such a threatening position? Mary Gage, a certified hypnotherapist, states: "What happens in hypnotherapy is the reprogramming of the messages in the subconscious mind."[7]

The relaxation techniques students are taught *are* hypnosis, as shown by the fact that they follow the basic principles of hypnosis:

Relaxation
Concentration
Suggestion
Repetition[8]

The Michigan Model of Comprehensive School Health Education, Problem Solving with People, follows the first three points.[9] Teachers are also advised:

Students need frequent, continuous practice in Problem-Solving with People, therefore, formal lessons are merely an introduction to procedures which are used *daily* throughout the elementary school experience, in both classroom and playground interactions. The chief value of the PSP process lies in its long-range benefit when students *automatically* apply thoughtful, problem-solving behaviors to situations at home and in the classroom.[10]

In addition, the teacher's goal is set forth: "Consequently, relevant aspects of the process should be utilized by teachers and other adults in the student's life whenever possible. This consistent approach is the best way to create problem-solving *habits* to replace more impulsive habits, which only make problems worse."[11]

Despite what teachers may have told parents, such programs do not consist of a few deep breaths. It is an educational equation that reads:

$$\text{Affective education} + \text{hypnotic technique} + \text{problem solving} = \text{reprogramming}$$

Problem Solving

In the end, students attempt to solve problems using the techniques of affective education. This method encourages them to be nonjudgmental and noncritical, but it does not provide insight. Teachers are told to keep everything "values neutral." No moral directives are part of the decision-making process.

At the heart of affective education is the process of valuing and decision making that bases right and wrong upon how a person feels. The courses Problem Solving With People, Group Decision Making, Social Problem Solving, or Values Clarification all provide a decision-making process of five to eleven steps that may vary slightly, but all perform the same function. In it, students are encouraged to:

1. Initiate calm (slow) breathing. Find the facts about what is happening right now.
2. Find out what happened before the problem situation. What might have led up to this situation?
3. Define the main problem.
4. Set a goal. What would be the best ending, what would be the worst?
5. What if we did this? Then what would happen? Determine solutions and consequences of those solutions.
6. Decide. Choose a plan of action and try it.
7. See if the goal was reached. If not, choose another action plan and try again.

Students do this exercise as a class, offer their solutions, and vote on the "best" one.

In such teaching, choice is deemed of more value than the law. Because of the nondirective technique used, nothing is designated illegal or immoral, thereby diluting moral decision making to a matter of preference.

Such problem solving does not teach students peer-resistance skills. Instead it reinforces the need for group consensus and approval. Students become dependent on their peers and increasingly value popularity and social acceptance as virtues, so it's not surprising that in real life they will go along with the crowd in drug or alcohol abuse or another illegal act.

By his or her silence, the teacher indicates agreement with whatever the class decides. Using such techniques places the reasoning ability and choice of a child on an equal plane with an adult's. When a child has been taught this in the school, it places him in direct conflict with his parents, if they disagree with that class's choice. In school he has learned the power of his class's decisions, and the idea that young people are less than all-powerful will come as a shock.

While once the parents would only have to deal with a child's rebellion, the class decision now has an adult authority figure—the teacher. Distrust and family division has been placed within the family by a respected person. For many teens, this will make the wrong option look right.

This form of problem solving assumes that young people can only make a right decision if adults do not impose their views on the process. It believes that children are basically good and will come up with a healthy decision as long as they are left alone. Those of us who believe that temptation exists and that people sin will have a hard time believing, as do such educators, that even if a child makes a poor decision, it will eventually be to his benefit, because he will have learned this truth by himself. We do not want our children to try drugs or commit suicide as a learning experience.

Results of Affective Education

A Dangerous Combination

The combination of role-playing and habits born of hypnosis can influence a child greatly:

> Dr. Ivan P. Pavlov was a Russian physiologist. He received the Nobel prize for physiology and medicine in 1904 for his outstanding contribution in tracing patterns of behavior based on laboratory research with animals. He was the first authority on the development of conditioned reflexes. In his experiments, he not only discovered how habits originate, but what makes them repetitive. Dr. Pavlov not only demonstrated that habits become entrenched by repetition; he also discovered something else. CONDITIONING IS STRONGER AND FASTER WHEN EMOTIONS ARE INVOLVED. Dr. Pavlov proved that a conditioned reflex (habit) could be established even from just one input if strong emotion is present. Because this is true, traumatic shocks can bring on reflexive behavior which may last a lifetime.[12]

Affective educational techniques have handed us a lit bomb, and we will only observe its potential for destruction in years to come.

By introducing role-playing into the school, educators produce stress. They place a child in situations she is developmentally incapable of handling. So naturally educators begin to perceive the need for stress reduction (hypnosis) in the classroom.

Imposing upon a child the decision about who should die in a crisis situation can only be likened to providing her with an imposed nightmare. As the title of the book edited by Phyllis Schlafly says, it is *Child Abuse in the Classroom.*[13]

The Influence on Teachers and Students

To the teacher with firm moral values, standing by while students come to erroneous decisions must be extremely frustrating. A teacher who loves her students and profession wants to help children avoid the wasted time, frustration, and perhaps the disciplinary action that come with making poor decisions.

With a younger child, the same teacher would quickly pass on the information, "You must never play with matches," to keep the child from harm. Yet here she is forced to let a teen make his own decision concerning the danger of drugs. By her enforced silence, the teacher implies that drug use is of less danger than lighting a fire.

Instead of passing on information—the central method of education—that teacher is directed to withhold it. Forced to use such techniques, she becomes as much a victim as the students are.

What does affective education do to students? Again Dr. Coulson tells us:

> Affective education turns kids into starters. The research is clear and consistent on this, with numerous studies yielding the same results: getting facilitation instead of teaching causes students to become more interested in making decisions than in doing what is right. . . . Youthful experimentation with sex, alcohol, marijuana, and a variety of other drugs—whatever is popular at the time—has been shown to follow affective, value free education quite predictably. We now know that after these classes, students become more prone to give into temptation than if they had never been enrolled. [14]

In other words, it causes affective-education students to experiment with anything. Children who receive such courses in sex-education or substance-abuse classes are worse off than those having had no instruction at all! The learning they took part in increased their likelihood of trying things and reduced their ability to resist inappropriate decisions. Those children apt to speak out most aggressively in this kind of education are the ones who have already begun the experimentation process. They frequently set the tone of discussion and classroom acceptance of behavior.

Imagine that Jim comes into class and tells his classmates about the "fun" he had getting drunk at a recent party. If the "nonjudgmental" teacher sits by silently, what will the other children think when Jim challenges them, "Hey, man, it didn't hurt me any, and I had a great time"? The child with strong traditional family values will face tremendous peer pressure to drink, and the experimenting child will have no chance to be turned from a destructive course.

Parental Response

In a 1978 article in *Parents* magazine, Richard A. Gardner, M.D., Associate Clinical Professor of Child Psychology at Columbia University, College of Physicians and Surgeons, stated: "In my opinion there is no question that therapy is a form of brainwashing. The therapist, whether covertly or overtly, imposes his values on his patients."

What do we want to see in our schools—education or indoctrination? I think the answer is clear to most parents. But how can they respond, if they discover that affective education is part of their child's schooling?

They need to address the following questions to the administration.

Who gave these people permission to perform an experimental medical procedure on my child?

Who assessed these children and made the diagnosis that they were in need of treatment?

What are the determining factors for starting therapy?

Why is the same treatment being given to all the children in the classroom?

What assessments are being made pre- and post-treatment and what are the long- and short-term goals of therapy?

What is it that is expected to be "made better" or changed in these children?

Are teachers, who receive an instructional course of approximately twenty-four hours or less on this topic, properly trained to do the job of a psychiatrist, an M.D., who has over ten years of highly specialized training in this field?

Who is accountable for those children who have been and will continue to be damaged by teachers' practicing medicine without a license or appropriate qualifications?

Used by permission of Janet Bierlein.

If a school discovers that a child has some psychiatric disturbance, it is the educators' role to contact the parents and let them know about the behavior that has caused them to judge that such care is needed. Then the parents should obtain the proper assistance from professionals. No educator has the right to usurp the parental role.

But increasingly schools *have* begun to take on parenting roles. Educators feel that parents are not fulfilling their jobs. When the door is left open for schools to take on parenting and psychotherapy roles, it can step in where parents should be. Moms and dads can only avoid such a situation by taking on their proper roles and discovering what teens are learning in school.

Action Plan for Parents

1. Have you noticed differences between the education you received and the one your children are receiving? Name some specific changes. Are these a part of affective education? Ask your child about sex-education courses and others that may fit these categories.

2. Have your children been missing out on some of the basics? How do you know? What would you like to see covered more completely? Talk to your child's teacher about this.

3. Are the parents in your child's school aware of the influence of affective education on the school system? If not, make an effort to educate them. If necessary, start a parents' group to encourage the school to return to traditional standards.

4. If your school uses affective education, plan to confront the administration by asking the questions outlined in this chapter. Seek to show administrators how such education can harm children and education. Help them plan a more effective course.

13
THE FLAWS IN AFFECTIVE EDUCATION

It's clear where a school system filled with affective education will take our children: into experimentation. If we stand by and let our teens only hear our silence, we have, in effect, condoned affective education's message. We present them with the messages that they are in no danger, or if they do face danger, we do not care about them enough to instruct them in the way they should live.

Parents need to understand the threat to their children and stand against it clearly. They need to see the subtle messages that are included in the sex-education and drug-education curricula and know how to counteract them.

The Flaw in Nondirective Education

Educators may tout the nondirective approach to education, but imagine the chaos it would create if we used the same system in the business world. Attempt to envision a job-training program in which no one told the trainees how to do things. How much nonproductive time would workers waste trying to come up with solutions and achieving only fail-

School Daze

ure? Yet some schools insist on training children for *life* with this system.

Suppose we required our doctors and scientists to rediscover every bit of knowledge that makes up their professional lives? How many incredible treatments and accomplishments we would miss!

It's the same with our children. How can we encourage them in ignorance, when we have knowledge to offer them? Do we really want our teens to feel more pain so that they can learn all these things for themselves?

I'm not advocating that teens not be able to make their own decisions, but I've seen too many fall into the "values neutral" trap laid by nondirective education. I've counseled with them when they're hurt because they ignored traditional morality and had to pay the price.

The sort of education we see in our schools often leads teens only to consider their own desires. They seem to remain ignorant of the fact that the way they live has an influence upon others. The act of sex involves two people—and it may hurt two people—but pregnancy affects three or more. We need to make teens aware of the dangers—clearly, without double messages that confuse them—and encourage them to take responsibility for their actions.

Sex Education Dangers

Let us not minimize the dangers of nondirective education about sex. It has taught our children:

> All things are chooseable.
> Sex is neither right nor wrong, as long as both parties make the decision to have it.
> More information about sex is equal to physical and emotional maturity.

In 1986 Lou Harris did a study for Planned Parenthood. To the dismay of that organization, he discovered that increased levels of sexual misconduct followed nondirective education.[1] But that has not caused all educators to remove it from the curriculum.

Unsuspecting parents and teens need to become aware of two subtle

146

methods nondirective education has used to change attitudes about sex from the traditional ones of yesterday to today's "anything goes" message.

Redefining Terms

Instead of encouraging children to change their behavior to suit moral values, nondirective education has taught them to redefine terms, in an effort to maintain social acceptability for their actions.

For example, some curricula define *monogamous* as "with one partner at a time." Such a definition makes it possible for a person to be "monogamous" with many partners, as long as he or she doesn't have them simultaneously.

Those who define *monogamous* this way have not read the primary definition of the word in *Webster's New Collegiate Dictionary:* "The practice of marrying only once during a lifetime." Nor have they heard the warning stated by Dr. Thomas E. Elkins, chief of gynecology at the University of Michigan, that having multiple sex partners in a lifetime is "probably the most important health risk factor for a young woman in America today."[2] As the rate of sexually active teens increases, so does the rate of sexually transmitted diseases and their side effects.

Limited Information

In the newest fad in some school systems, beginning in kindergarten children receive information on AIDS, through the reproductive health curriculum. Many states have gone so far as to mandate such education. My own passed this law: "The principal modes by which dangerous communicable diseases, including, but not limited to, acquired immunodeficiency syndrome, are spread and the best methods for the restriction and prevention of these diseases shall be taught in every public school in this state."[3]

Like many parents, I am not concerned about the necessity to teach about the dangers of AIDS. What does concern me is the information that students are receiving.

Most curricula nowhere state that homosexuality is wrong or even that students should avoid it for their own safety. Because the writers of these programs have wanted to avoid harsh treatment for victims of AIDS, they have passed onto our young people a dangerously limited message. As a result, I believe many children will feel safe experimenting with homosexual sex and will find themselves in a life-threatening situation.

By attempting to be "values neutral" about homosexuality, curricula have avoided presenting these statistics: According to the Centers for Disease Control statistics, 65 percent of those with AIDS have a homosexual life-style; 21 percent obtained the virus through IV drug use. Only 5 percent of those with AIDS had a heterosexual life-style, and the CDC states that in heterosexual transmission: "These cases result from heterosexual contact with people in known risk groups."[4]

In other words, cases that involved heterosexual sex can be traced back to a homosexual or bisexual partner, an IV drug user, or someone who received a contaminated blood product. Though homosexuals make up only 3 percent of the population, they account for 65 percent of the AIDS victims.

But what happens in our schoolrooms?

> Even though statistics continue to show the number one risk factor for the transmission of AIDS is the passage of infected semen into the rectum of homosexual partners, it is never stated in the curriculum. The curriculum for Junior and Senior High students should clearly state that promiscuous male homosexual activity and IV drug use are the major means of transmission for the AIDS virus and are potentially harmful. Further, a reproductive health curriculum should deal with reproduction. Homosexuals cannot reproduce and their activities should not be a part of the curriculum.[5]

Why are these truths being hidden from our teens? Why don't they hear that AIDS lasts a lifetime—and it's a very short lifetime, once you show symptoms of the disease!

The limitation of information does not only appear when the subject is AIDS. Educators give our children a limited message on other sexual dangers. Dr. Elkins reports that it has become routine to see "precancerous and early cancerous lesions between the ages of 17–35. . . . Persons with 2–5 sexual partners in their lifetime had a 3.4 times relative risk for developing cervical cancer over a person with only one person in a lifetime. Six or more partners in a lifetime revealed a 5 times greater risk to the person involved than that of a person with only one partner in a lifetime."[6] But how many sex-education courses provide such a warning?

Those who take part in numerous sexual experiences with multiple partners have reduced sex to anatomical and biological functions performed in the absence of a lifelong commitment. Emotionally, this places the emphasis on the wants of the individual, not the essence of sex as being just one part of a larger relationship. Along with many sex therapists, psychiatrists, and physicians at a Cleveland Clinic seminar, Dr. Joseph LoPiccolo noted,

> The most prominent sexual dysfunction being seen today throughout the country, is the loss of sexual desire. . . . It is often a sense of boredom with the sexual act that is eroding the marriages and relationships of many within our society. It is fascinating that the treatment for this is teaching to learn how to communicate again, how to care, how to commit to one another. It appears that these things may have been forgotten in their rush to learn how to have sex "safely" and with a great deal of "fun" and "enjoyment."[7]

The Need for Change

I don't believe most parents want their children to experience the kind of hurt doctors Elkins and LoPiccolo describe. However, by ignoring the affective-education message, "Try it!" parents place themselves in the position of raising children who will experiment.

A July 1989 *Life* magazine article portrayed teen sexuality. Though one teen showed herself as being more conservative than her mother, in most cases, young people reflected the message that sex was something they should take part in. Some parents went so far as providing their teens with condoms. In their sex-education classes, those teens hear, "Say no . . . but if you can't say no, then use a condom!"

We can give our teens a better message than that. Someone needs to point out the truths that:

God says that premarital or extramarital sex is wrong.
AIDS lasts for a lifetime—a short lifetime.
Low self-esteem accompanies the loss of a lover.

Women who experience an abortion may also experience the trauma—mentally and emotionally—that follows the death of that baby.

Until teens hear these and other truths about the dangers of sex, how can they make a sensible choice?

A Parental Response

At this point, surely some parents are begging to ask their school administrators these questions:

Why would schools continually use a method that has failed so greatly?

How can educators think they are serving the best interests of the children by encouraging them to learn these things?

Why would parents want their children to take part in a program that encourages them in sexual activity, when it is so dangerous physically and emotionally?

I believe these are all questions educators need to hear, though they may not relish them. Unless parents confront teachers and administrators, there is no hope of change.

But parents may also receive a fairly hostile response, because educators are not always encouraged to think well of them. In the next chapter, we'll take a look at educational stereotypes of parents as reflected in educational literature. We'll also take a look at the books that encourage ideas that go against parental authority.

Action Guide for Parents

1. Have you silently condoned the message of affective education in your child's life? How can you change that? Create an action plan.

2. Review your child's sex-education materials. Do they give the three dangerous messages described above? How do they redefine terms and limit information? Do you notice anything else that opposes a traditional morality?

3. If your child's sex-education program has a nondirective approach, contact the school system. Ask them some of the questions in this chapter, along with some of your own. Then consider how you can work effectively to change the influences of such education on your child. Is the school open to change? Can your child opt out of the program?

4. If your school is not open to changing a nondirective program, are parents aware of the impact this teaching has on their children? Contact a few to see if you can encourage a move for change.

14

CHALLENGING PARENTHOOD

Being a parent today is a challenging task. The pressures our teens face become our pressures. When our children receive bad messages, we cannot close our eyes and ignore them.

Though many teachers are truly concerned for teens and want to do their best for them, often they have been taught that they need to fill a void left by parents. If they begin to see that parents do not take an active part in their children's education, teachers may also believe the negative messages given to them by some educators and education literature. For example, the Michigan Model for Comprehensive School Health Education portrays parents as uncaring, selfish, abusing, alcoholic, on drugs, having dangerous smoking habits, and so on.[1]

Not only do those who feel this way pass on that idea to other educators, their attitudes filter down to students. Teachers may challenge a parent's authority, encourage a child to defy his family's traditional values, or otherwise give a child the idea that it's okay to experiment.

Honoring Parents or Challenging Them?

Recently my brother, Dale, shared the curriculum for his son's eighth-grade human development/sex-education program with me. Dale had decided to take part and look into the program before he agreed to let his son take it. How glad I am that my brother did this!

In "Uncle Henry's Advice Column," a part of this curriculum, a teen had written a letter asking Uncle Henry to get her father to change her curfew, because he was ruining her social life by making her come home by midnight.[2] Nothing in the curriculum encourages that teen to respect her parents, and in a nondirective-education environment it is unlikely that anyone will encourage students to consider that her parents care for her and want the best for her. Just about every teen thinks Mom and Dad are ruining her social life, but that does not mean that those parents are wrong or that they do not care for her. Yet this probably will never be the message she hears.

In another part of the curriculum, eight out of forty-one pages are spent telling the story of Baby X, which subtly tells young teens that there are no sexual differences. The parents of this child do not want to treat it like either a boy or girl, because they don't want to influence it one way or another. The story portrays the Parent Committee—which stands for most parents—as insensitive, while Baby X's parents are acclaimed for the wonderful job they have done. The homosexual life-style is portrayed as being vastly superior to the normal heterosexual one.

By showing teens that their parents are incompetent and have hopelessly "old-fashioned" ideas, teachers can undermine parental authority. What teen doesn't want to be "cool"? How many teens of caring moms and dads think their parents are "cool"? It's natural for a teen to think his parents are impossible, but when a school condones such thinking, much family conflict may result.

In another exercise, teens vote on questions that range from how late a teen should be allowed to stay out on a date to whether or not virginity is outdated.[3] Suppose a class of teens voted that living together before marriage was perfectly fine. How many responsible teens would be willing to court others' disapproval by objecting, "But the Bible says . . . ," or, "My parents have taught me . . ."? Even if a teen *did* have the courage to speak out in class and withstand the giggling, what will he encounter outside the class?

What girl will be willing to stand up in class and say, "I believe we should wait until marriage to have sex," when she fears it will mean she'll never be asked on a date?

Perhaps you have told your teen to wait until he's older to date, but in a sex-ed class a street-smart student says, "I think we should be able to choose when we date. I don't think parents should have anything to say about it. Besides, look at me. I'm in the eighth grade, and I've been dating for three years. It hasn't hurt me!" Won't your son feel tempted to go against your will? Take it from someone who works with teens day in and day out—it *will* influence your teen.

How can all this peer pressure affect the shy teen, the quiet one? If she is harassed in class—or out of it—how long will it take her to get over that? When a teacher does not stop students from picking on her in class or her classmates belittle her during lunch or after school, she may learn to fear taking part. Remember, teachers are only facilitators and can't go against the students' ideas, only record them. If your child can't stand up clearly for her own decision and hold fast to it, such abuse could have a lifetime impact upon her. If she does hold fast, the harassment may increase.

The message peer accountability implies is "You aren't really responsible to Mom and Dad; *we* are more important in your life." Teens who spend their lives trying to win the approval of others will never develop a firm moral foundation.

Sending Teens a Different Message

Like most parents, you probably don't want your teen to become an experimenter. But if you leave your son or daughter only with the message that an affective education sex-ed course provided, you'll encourage that. My nephew's school's curriculum for sex education *did* offer children the option of abstinence, but only after many pages describing the joy of sex. It also portrayed using a condom as a caring act. Once a child has learned these things, why will he turn away from sex? How can he believe that it's wrong?

It is critical that parents become aware of the literature their children read in and out of the classroom. Most sex-education materials will reflect a nondirective approach and will give teens a mixed message that actually encourages sex. While such materials may at one point or another imply that it's also okay to avoid sex, it will give graphic sexual information, such as how to put on a condom.

Let's take a look at how we can evaluate the materials children receive in a course.

Evaluating the School's Message

My friend Otto Moulton, from the Committees of Correspondence, Inc., alerted me to some of the dangers in a book entitled *Saying No Is Not Enough,* by Robert Schwebel, Ph.D. The subtitle reads, "Raising Children Who Make Wise Decisions About Drugs and Alcohol—The Positive Prevention Guide for Parents," and it is introduced by Dr. Benjamin Spock.

This book is widely used in schools and prevention programs. From the title, most parents would imagine it was just what they were looking for. But open the book and look carefully at its message, and you may want to reconsider.

Otto calls it, "A good example of bad information."

Saying No Is Not Enough uses reference material by self-proclaimed advocates of drug legalization, and it does not clearly state that all drug use is abuse and illegal for minor children. Also, it contains what Otto calls "dangerously incorrect information on the issue of whether or not a user can stop. It is stated on page 34, 'Drug use can stop at any stage.' Most addiction-treatment professionals can disprove this, based on the statements of the users they treat."

The book also includes this statement: "Most teenagers who use drugs do not develop lasting problems." That is incorrect and dangerous. The majority of adolescent-treatment professionals, in programs around the country, could disprove this statement. (*See also* Appendix II.)

According to Otto, much of the research in *Saying No Is Not Enough* comes from 1979 and has since been discredited. Dr. Spock was a board member of the National Organization for the Reform of Marijuana Laws (NORML), which advocates marijuana legalization. The book was greatly influenced by the writings of Andrew Weil, a leader in the drug culture. He, too, is on the board of NORML and writes articles for *High Times* magazine. He is pro-drugs, and that is the direction in which he devotes his energies.

When the Committees of Correspondence evaluates drug prevention material, they use the following criteria. I have shown their rating of each on the book *Saying No Is Not Enough.* (A rating of 1 is poor, and 5 is excellent.)

1. *Is It a Current Publication?* This book received a 4. It was the highest rating the book got in any of the eighteen areas. We can at least say the book was current.
2. *Bibliography—Creditable Reference:* It was rated 1. The references were not creditable. The book has an agenda of getting children to use drugs.
3. *Appropriate to Age Level:* The book received a 3.
4. *Presumption of Non-use:* Because the book did not presume children would not use drugs, it received a 1.
5. *Promotes Positive Standards of Behavior; Use Is Wrong, Harmful, Illegal and Non-use Is Right, Healthy and Legal:* This also received a 1 rating, because the book does not come out and say that drug use is wrong, harmful, or illegal.
6. *Outlines Realistic Consequences:* This received a −1, because the book several times stated that the consequences were no big deal, that kids could probably stop any time, and the effects would stop as well.
7. *Accurate Information on the Effects of Drugs on the Brain and Body:* This received a 3 rating.
8. *Short-term and Long-term Effects Are Listed:* This received a 2 rating.
9. *Unique, Harmful Nature of Each Drug Is Noted:* They did that, but not very strongly, so the rating was 2.
10. *Alcohol Is Included as an Illegal Drug for Minors:* The book received a rating of 1 because it did not say alcohol was illegal for minors.
11. *Positive, Healthy Role Models Are Displayed:* The rating here was N/A (Not Applicable), because there weren't any.

12. *Message Is Clear and Consistent:* The message was not consistent, so the book received a 2 rating.

13. *Avoids History of Drugs, Reasons for Doing Drugs, and Responsible Use Concepts:* Received a 1 rating.

14. *Teaches "No Use" Techniques and Refusal Skills:* This got a 1 rating.

15. *Studies Addiction and Addiction Process With Emphasis on Empowering Non-Users to Help Users:* Received a 1 rating.

16. *Includes the Relationship of Drugs to AIDS:* Received a 1 rating.

17. *Family, Teacher, Police, etc. Are Resources for Assistance:* The book did not encourage that. It got a 1 rating.

18. *Resource Materials are Up-to-date, Accurate, Protective of Children and Pro-Parent:* Received a 1 rating.

You can use these concepts to evaluate the literature your school recommends or provides for your child. Use them as a basis for creating your own checklist for books on AIDS and sex, too. By carefully reading and evaluating your child's material, you may save him the heartbreak of too many mistakes or one mistake that bills him.

As you begin to look at your child's books, you'll probably begin to realize that I've not exaggerated the dangers. I spend much of my time in schools. I love our teens and want the best for them. Therefore I have not attempted to use scare tactics. When I first heard about the dangers of affective education, I thought people had exaggerated. But as I began to check things out for myself, I ran into concepts that clearly were harmful to our teens.

We don't want to send to our children the message that they're uncared for by Mom and Dad, that they are not important—even to God. But in order to help them hear the true message, we must seek to have the schools reflect our traditional values. We need to hold them accountable for what they are saying and the kind of results that can be seen in our children's lives.

Most parents love their children more than anyone else—except God. Child-abuse situations exist, but they are not part of the lives of most students. We cannot let the minority situation govern the entire school.

Parents need to take a stand. After all, their taxes pay the salaries of teachers, administrators, and other staff members and keep our schools going. Those who pay have a right to say what occurs in the classroom. But unless we are willing to take a stand, that will never happen.

I know you don't want to fight any more than I do. When I consider going into my children's school and confronting the principal on such issues, I get nervous. My palms feel sweaty just as I think about a confrontation, because I don't want one.

I'd prefer to enjoy my life and be at ease. I've worked hard, and I want to reach my own kids, play with them, run my business, enjoy an occasional sport, and save up money for my golden years. But if I don't fight, who will? Can I afford to let my own children—and others—pay the price with diseases, bad memories, and pain? I don't think so. So I have to take action, even when it's hard.

Parental Action

I would encourage you, too, to take part in this offensive against an immoral life-style for our children. But before you start, take an accounting of your situation. Be aware that this project will continue for at least as long as you have school-age children—maybe even longer. So pace yourself and your expectations for the long haul. Up front, consider your own foundations. Look at what you would like to achieve, what you will tolerate, and what you will not. You may also want to consider your legal options. Understand what the law says about this situation, so that you can react responsibly.

Then be ready to hang in there for the long haul. Your commitment and perseverance will speak more loudly than your words.

You may want to become active in your school in the following ways:

1. Participate in school board meetings and committees.
2. Make your child's teacher aware of your concerns regarding the lack of foundational morals being taught or supported.
3. Review the curriculum and books your child will be utilizing for the upcoming year. Be familiar with them. Investigate what is being taught in your child's classroom and hold the teacher accountable.
4. Alert your school's curriculum committee to any materials you

find that are objectionable and be sure to explain why you object.

5. Follow through. Check back with the school to see what changes have been made as a result of your criticisms.

6. Seek out a position on the curriculum committee of your school.

7. Be a room parent and participate, when you can, in the education of your child.

8. Be a member of your school's reproductive health advisory committee.

9. Run for a position on your school board.

As you take part in your school, keep in mind these guidelines:

1. When you present information, be certain you have done your homework. If you use resources, what bias do they have? Are they technically accurate? Know the basis you are speaking from, so you can respond to questions.

2. Treat others with respect. Even when you disagree with another board member, do so tactfully and kindly. If you do not turn every issue into a fight, you will gain the respect of others and have a greater impact for good upon your school system.

3. Understand your own limitations. You may not have expertise in a certain area. To speak effectively on an issue, you may need to admit that. If possible, find someone else who does have knowledge in that area and work with that expert. Encourage others to become part of your team.

The goal of changing the schools is not impossible. Most school administrators are sensitive to the need to respond to the community. But the only way they can know what the community feels is if parents let them *know*.

Become active in your schools. It will help your teens—and those around them.

Action Plan for Parents

1. Talk to your child's teacher or guidance counselor. What does he or she think of parents? How have experiences influenced that opinion?

Have you had a part in creating such an opinion? Are you different from that idea? How? What can you do to give that teacher or counselor a better opinion of parents?

2. How does your teen's school literature undermine your parenting role? Reinforce it? How much does your teen experience peer pressure to turn away from your teachings?

3. How can you send your teen a different message about right and wrong, respect for authority, and experimentation with sex and drugs? Come up with creative ways you can present a different message. Can you talk about it? Share your ideas with a group of his friends? Give her a book that challenges her to seek the best for her life? How can you help your teen not become confused by the differences between messages received at school and home?

4. Are you aware of the kinds of literature your teen is encouraged to read in school? Do you know of some books that could encourage him to better values? Take a look at books that are available at the local library, secular bookstore, and Christian bookstore. How do they differ? Do you agree with their message? Why or why not? Which ones can you recommend to your child?

5. How can you become active in your school? Set out an action plan that includes other parents, school boards, or regular school functions. Take part *actively* in what's going on around you.

Appendix I
TEEN SURVEY
RESULTS

In Part II: A Teen's-Eye View of Life, we considered the major results of my survey of 7,500 teens in the seventh through twelfth grades. Here are the more complete statistics. Percentages may be more or less than 100 percent since in some cases I asked for more than one answer, and in others I did not receive an answer to every question.

Though teens answered differently, often the emotions or experiences behind those responses were similar. What came through clearly was that teens *want* to communicate with their parents. They want support, and they want to learn from them. While they may put up a tough front, our children hurt inside.

Often teens seemed to lack the analytical abilities to figure where the relationship with Mom and Dad went wrong and what they could do to help. Even when they could tell me what was wrong, many seemed unable to identify how they could improve things.

Parents need to focus on the people skills teens need to learn. At home is the best place to learn about how people get along well with one another. So few of our children know how to do that, but they *can* learn to do it as we show them the way.

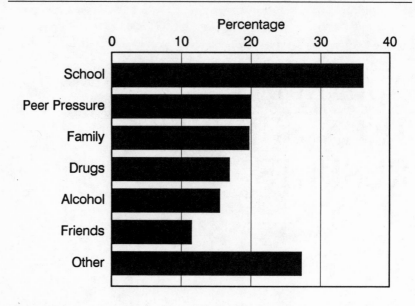

What are the greatest problems you face?

School/grades/homework	36.2%
Peer pressure	20.0%
Parents/family	19.7%
Drugs	16.9%
Alcohol	15.5%
Peers/friends	11.5%
Sex	9.2%
Dating/boyfriend or girlfriend	8.8%
Money/job	7.6%
Fitting in/popularity	4.7%

When I asked for the three greatest problems teens faced, pressure to achieve and pressure from peers ranked high on their list. Often the pressure to achieve comes from parents (or teachers). But with both adults and their friends, teens have pressure-cooker relationships. Along with the pressures, teens need to learn coping mechanisms.

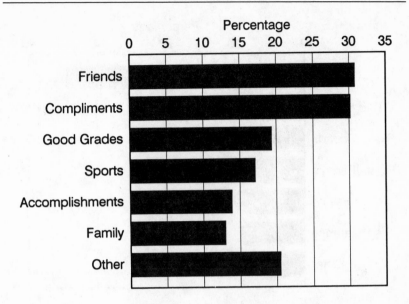

What helps you feel good about yourself and builds up your self-esteem?

Friends	30.8%
Compliments	30.2%
Good grades	19.4%
Sports	17.1%
Accomplishments/success	13.9%
Parents/family	13.0%
Dating/boyfriend or girlfriend	8.7%
Helping others	5.0%
Communicating	3.5%
Fitting in/being accepted	3.3%

Asked for three things that made them feel good about themselves, teens largely focused on relationships and accomplishments. But relationships seem to give teens more of a boost, because they appeared here so heavily, in many different forms, from helping others to making good grades.

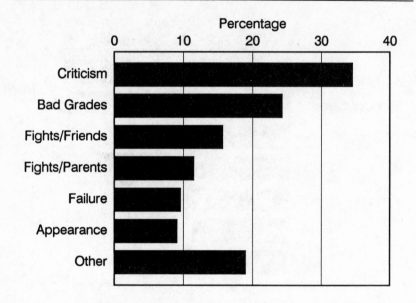

What are some things that make you feel depressed and have a lousy self-esteem?

Criticism/being teased	34.6%
Bad grades	24.3%
Fighting with friends	15.7%
Fighting with parents	11.5%
Failure	9.6%
Appearance	9.1%
Dating/boyfriend or girlfriend	7.4%
Being left out/lonely	6.6%
Losing/doing bad in sports	5.0%

The things that made teens feel bad about themselves were a reversal of what made them feel good; again they focused on relationships and accomplishments.

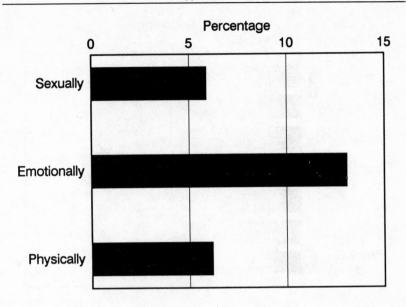

Have you ever been abused?

19.0% said yes
  5.9%—Sexually
  13.1%—Emotionally
  6.2%—Physically

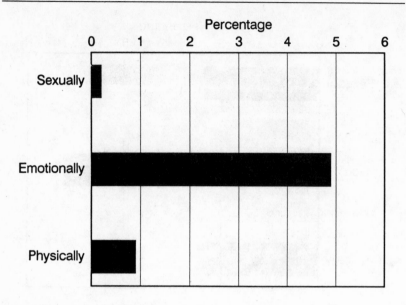

Are you being abused now?

5.5% said yes
  .2%—Sexually
  4.9%—Emotionally
  .9%—Physically

Here are some of the saddest statistics that came out of my survey. Nearly a fifth of our teens admitted to experiencing some sort of abuse. I have to wonder how many of those teens are still being abused and did not have the courage to admit it.

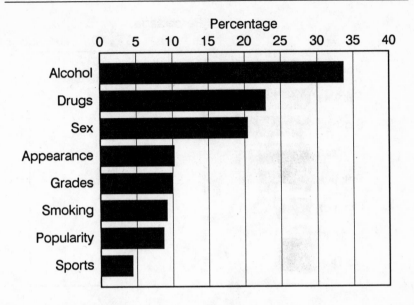

What are the three largest pressures put on you by your peers?

Alcohol	33.7%
Drugs	22.9%
Sex	20.4%
Appearance/clothes	10.2%
School/grades	10.0%
Smoking	9.2%
Fitting in/popularity	8.7%
Sports	4.4%

Twenty percent of our teens admitted that peer pressure was one of their greatest problems. When I specifically asked about the pressures put on teens by peers, over 55 percent had been pressured to use drugs and alcohol. Another 20 percent had been pressured to have sex. Teens may be able to stand up against the "need" to wear the latest styles, but how can they easily stand up against the favorite pastimes of their fellow students? The fact that such stringent pressure to do moral wrong exists shows us how far we have fallen away from a biblical morality and how influential the pressures of affective education have become.

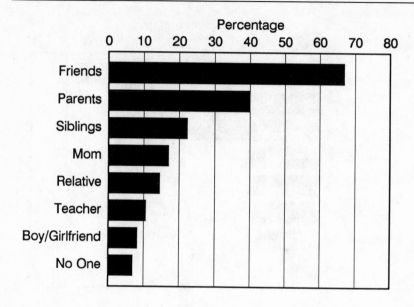

Whom do you go to for advice?

Friends	66.9%
Parents	39.9%
Siblings	22.2%
Mom	17.0%
Relative/family	14.5%
Teacher	10.6%
Boyfriend/girlfriend	8.2%
No one else/myself	6.9%

When it comes to advice, given the opportunity to fill in three sources, friends came out heavily in the front, but parents or Mom came out well, too. Though parents may not be the *only* source of information, they do play a key role in many teens' opinion making. As they feel secure in asking Mom and Dad questions, teens are more likely to go to them for advice.

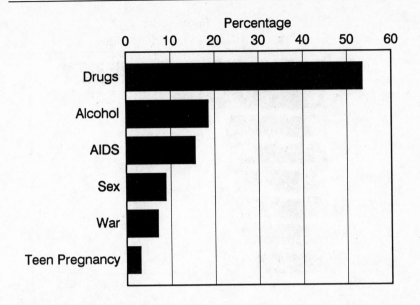

In your opinion, what is the largest problem facing America today?

Drugs	53.6%
Alcohol	18.6%
AIDS	15.6%
Sex	8.9%
War/Iraq	7.1%
Teen Pregnancy	3.1%

I asked this question at the height of the conflict with Iraq, but teens seemed less worried about the future of the world than the influence drugs and alcohol had on America. They've seen some of the damage drugs and alcohol cause, and they face its pressures—often every day.

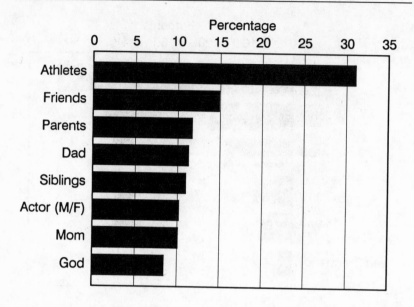

Who are your heroes?

Athletes/sports stars	31.1%
Friends	14.9%
Parents	11.7%
Dad	11.3%
Siblings	11.0%
Actors/actresses	10.2%
Mom	10.1%
God	8.5%
Musicians	7.8%
Michael Jordan	6.8%
Cartoon characters	6.3%

Teens had a wide variety of heroes, with the greatest number being sports stars. The good news is that our teens seem to have a variety of interests—and Mom and Dad both made it on the list. In view of the lack of morality in the lives of many superstars, that's a much needed balance. Don't be afraid, parents, to speak out on right and wrong.

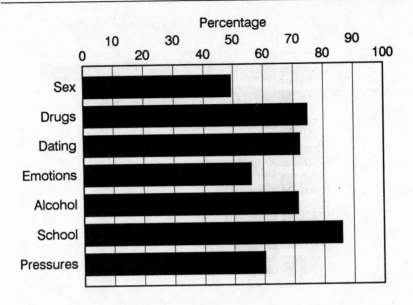

Do you feel you can talk to your parents about these important issues?

	Yes	*No*	*No Answer*
Sex	49.3%	48.3%	2.4%
Drugs	74.8%	23.5%	1.7%
Dating	72.2%	25.8%	2.0%
Emotions	55.9%	41.4%	2.7%
Alcohol	71.5%	26.7%	1.8%
School	86.2%	12.1%	1.7%
Pressures	60.3%	36.7%	3.0%

Teens can talk to their parents about some things—86.2 percent said they could talk about school. Moms and dads who want to improve communication need to build on the areas in which they already communicate. As Mom and Dad share their own lives, their teens can begin to open up.

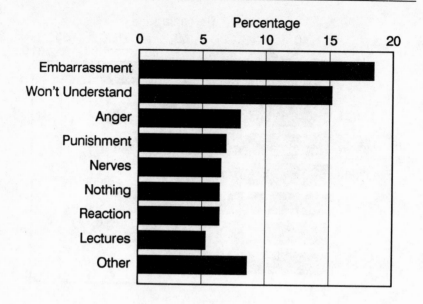

What keeps you from talking to your parent/parents about tough issues?

Embarrassment	18.5%
They won't understand	15.2%
Anger	8.0%
Punishment	6.9%
Scared/nervous	6.5%
Nothing/we communicate well	6.4%
Don't know their reaction	6.4%
Lecture/yell	5.3%
They won't listen	4.3%
Time/don't see them much	4.3%

Teens were less forthcoming on this question than on some others. Asked to describe three things that keep them from talking to parents, they gave me a list of fears. Parents who simply instill fear in their teens will not communicate well.

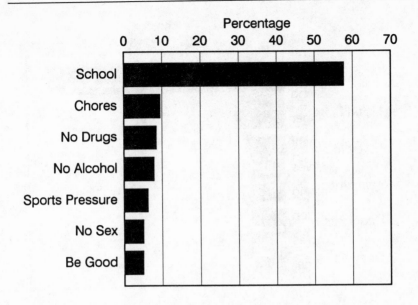

What are the three greatest pressures put on you by your parents?

School/grades/homework	57.8%
Chores	9.6%
No drugs	8.5%
No alcohol	7.9%
Sports/be a good athlete	6.3%
No sex	5.1%
Be good/stay out of trouble	5.0%

Notice that teens feel more pressure to get good grades than they do to complete chores or not to do drugs. What message are they receiving?

We push our children to do well, but we don't give them the basic tools to do well. How many of us clearly pass on the messages that they should help at home and should not do drugs? Then are we teaching them a broad range of people skills that will help them avoid peer pressure and become a success? Let's provide teens with messages that will show them the way to fruitful lives.

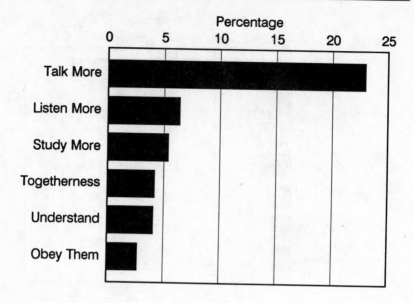

What could you do to meet your parents halfway and communicate more effectively?

Communicate/talk more	23.0%
Listen	6.4%
School/study more/better grades	5.4%
More time with them/do things together	4.2%
Understand them	4.1%
Obey them	2.7%

Less than half our teens could provide me with ways in which they could communicate more effectively with their parents. How are we training our children to relate to others? Perhaps some of our teens do not feel they need to communicate better with their parents and did not answer this question, but at least some hurting teens don't seem to have a clue as to how they could improve communication.

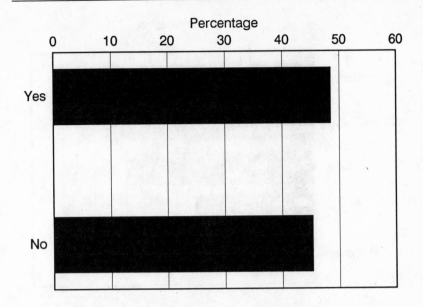

Do your parents say one thing and do another?

Yes	48.5%
No	45.3%
Sometimes	.8%
Did not answer this question	5.4%

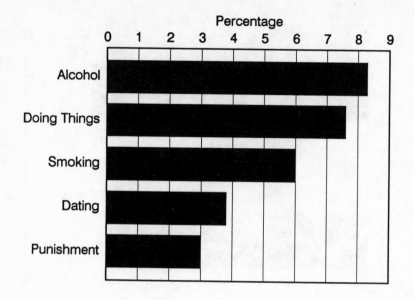

In what areas?

Alcohol	8.3%
Going places/doing things	7.6%
Smoking	6.0%
Dating	3.8%
Punishment	3.0%
Chores/housework	2.5%
Swearing	1.8%

Many teens—almost half—perceive that their parents say one thing and do another. Asked to identify the areas in which their parents failed, teens were not particularly forthcoming. Either many students perceive it as a natural part of life—perhaps they know we all sometimes fail—or they see such habitual hypocrisy that they find it hard to explain.

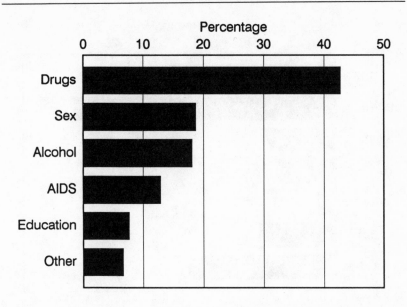

What pressures do you face today that your parents never faced?

Drugs	42.8%
Sex	18.7%
Alcohol	18.1%
AIDS	12.9%
Tougher schools/higher education/college	7.7%
Peer pressure	4.5%
Fitting in/popularity	2.2%

Teens definitely think they have it harder than their parents when it comes to drugs. Asked to identify three pressures they felt their parents could not relate to, over 40 percent named drugs, and another 18 percent identified alcohol. How many moms and dads have shared with their teens how they learned to say no to drugs? How many parents who have made a mistake can honestly tell their teens, "I never should have had a drink, and now I wish I hadn't"?

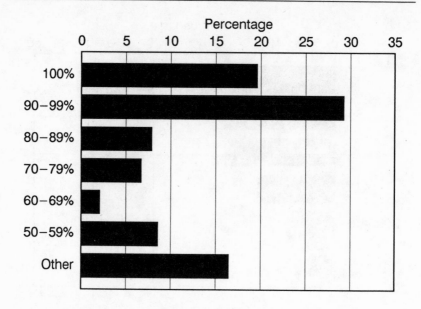

How often do your parents know what you do on the weekends?

100% of the time	19.6%
90–99%	29.3%
80–89%	7.9%
70–79%	6.7%
60–69%	2.1%
50–59%	8.6%
40–49%	2.2%
30–39%	1.3%
20–29%	2.6%
10–19%	3.5%
1–9%	3.4%
0%	3.5%
No answer	9.2%

Many parents seem to know where their teens are a large portion of the time. But how many of the lower percentages reflect parents who care but do not want to know too much about their teens' activities, for fear they'd need to express disapproval? When parents do disapprove, they need to dialogue with their teens. This is a great communication and teaching opportunity.

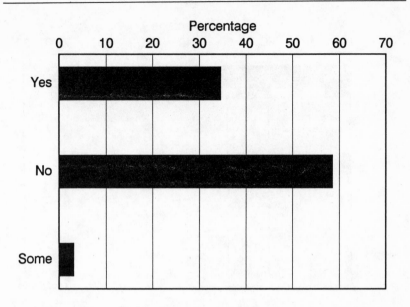

Do you lie to your parents about what you do on weekends?

Yes	34.6%
No	58.5%
Sometimes	3.2%
No answer	3.7%

Since almost half of our teens saw their parents as hypocrites, perhaps it's not surprising that at least a third of them sometimes lie to their parents about weekend activities. But the good news is that almost 60 percent of our teens are honest with us on this subject.

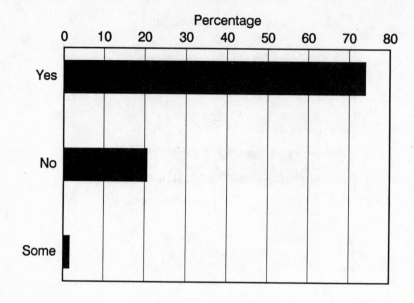

Do they ask you about your weekend activities?

Yes	74.1%
No	20.6%
Sometimes	1.6%
No answer	3.7%

Teens are aware that their parents have some interest in their weekend activities. Almost three-quarters of them said their parents asked. It's up to Mom and Dad to become a caring resource for teens when they plan their activities. Don't harshly dictate what can be done, but have a firm input on the wisdom of any activity that could do your teen harm.

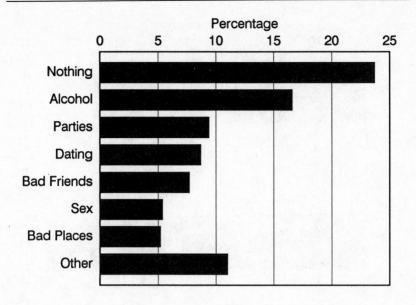

What are you doing on the weekends that you feel you must hide?

Nothing	23.7%
Alcohol	16.6%
Parties	9.4%
Dating	8.7%
With friends I shouldn't be with	7.7%
Sex	5.4%
Going places I'm not suppose to	5.2%
Out past curfew/Sneaking out	4.2%
Drugs	3.6%
Cruising	3.2%

Despite the facts that many teens did not lie to Mom and Dad, they often felt they had to hide something. If most parents are asking about a teen's weekend activities, perhaps they are not tuned into what the teen is saying, or maybe they just ask surface questions. Shallow relationships will consist of a quick question as a teen charges out the door. Spend time together. Plan some family activities. Make yours a deep, growing relationship.

Percentage

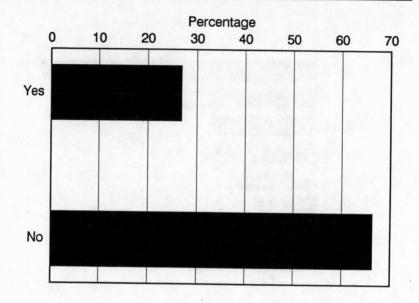

Have your parents ever called to see if your parties were chaperoned, and so on?

Yes	26.9%
No	66.4%
No answer	6.7%

Another way parents can show younger teens they care is to check up on their parties. As both teen and parents know this will happen, trust will be built and the need to act responsibly will be encouraged.

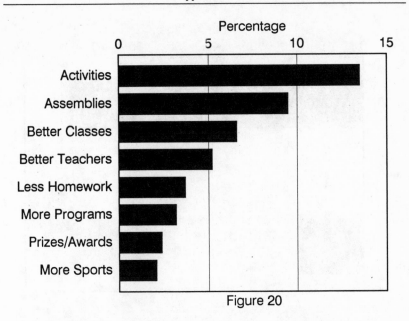

Figure 20

What could our schools do to get you motivated?

Activities/dances/field trips	13.5%
Assemblies/speakers	9.5%
Better classes/more exciting classes	6.6%
Better teachers/teachers who care	5.2%
Less homework	3.7%
More programs/clubs/drug education	3.2%
Prizes/awards	2.4%
More sports	2.1%

Only a minority of students felt the schools had to do something to further motivate them, and the concerns they expressed focused less on the academic side of school life than the social side.

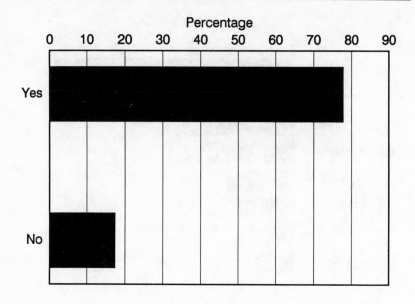

Do your teachers challenge you enough?

Yes	77.8%
No	17.5%
Sometimes	.6%
No answer	4.1%

Over three-quarters of our students felt they were challenged enough by their schools. While parents seem to feel their children need tougher educational standards, teens do not feel the need for more academic challenges.

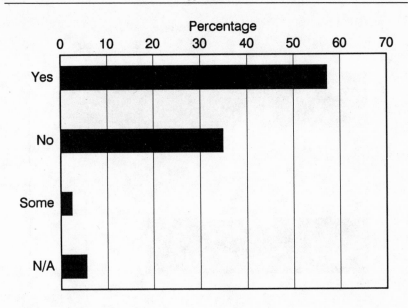

Do your teachers seem to care for you personally?

Yes	57.2%
No	34.9%
Somewhat	2.4%
No answer	5.5%

More than half the teachers got a good grade when it came to personal relationships. There are many caring teachers in our schools. We need to help them do a better job by keeping in touch with them, encouraging them, and supporting them at home.

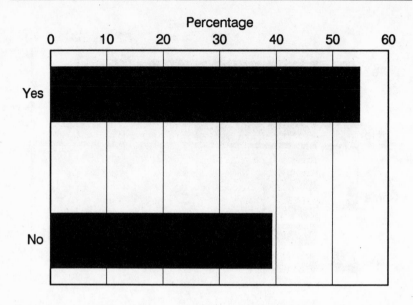

Do your parents visit your school during the year?

Yes	54.9%
No	39.3%
Sometimes	.5%
No answer	5.3%

Just more than half the students indicated their parents visited their schools. How many of those visited just once? Naturally it's frustrating for teachers who care about their students when they have no input from the home. How can they know why a student does poorly, excels, or doesn't come to class, if parents never contact them?

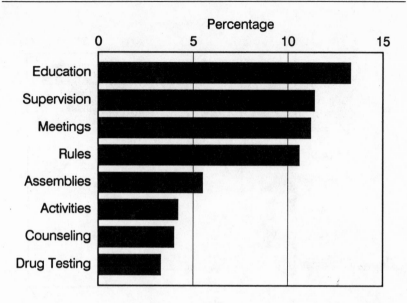

What could your school do to fight the drug and alcohol problem?

Educate/teach kids to say no	13.3%
Check lockers/search kids/watch more	11.4%
Groups/meetings/SADD/clubs	11.2%
Stricter rules and punishments	10.6%
Speakers/assemblies	5.5%
More nondrug activities	4.2%
Counseling/help kids/talk to them	4.0%
Drug tests	3.3%

Asked to name three ways in which schools could help fight drugs and alcohol, many teens seemed at a loss. Even if every student had provided me with only one answer, I would not have heard from over a third of them—and I'm certain some students gave me multiple answers. Parents and teachers must band together to provide teens with the help they need—a firm message that says, "Drugs and alcohol are not okay!"

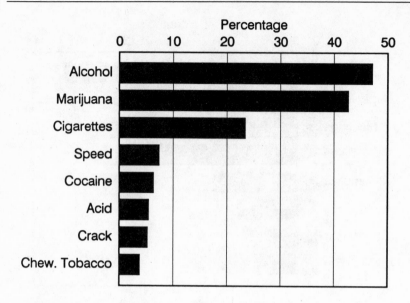

What drugs are in the largest use among students in your school?

Alcohol	47.2%
Marijuana	42.7%
Cigarettes	23.4%
Speed/uppers	7.4%
Cocaine	6.4%
Acid	5.5%
Crack	5.3%
Chewing tobacco	3.8%

Alcohol and marijuana—which many people see as "safe" drugs—are clearly the greatest threats to our young people. Asked to identify the three drugs in largest use in their schools, these came to the top over 40 percent of the time. Parents and teachers need to provide a strong message that indicts even the drugs that seem to cause little harm—at first.

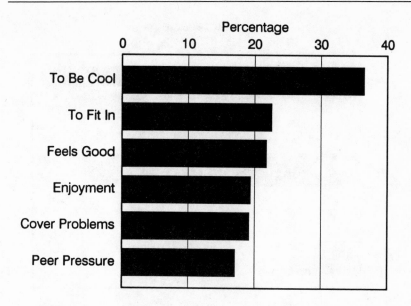

Why do you feel students drink alcohol?

To be cool	36.5%
To fit in	22.6%
Feels good to be drunk/buzzed	21.8%
Fun/enjoyment	19.4%
Cover up problems	19.2%
Peer pressure	17.1%

Asked to identify the three reasons they felt students used alcohol, teens came up with a long list of peer pressure excuses. If you add "to be cool," "to fit in," and "peer pressure," you have the reasons well over three-quarters of them drink. Sadly, over a fifth of our students seemed to identify feeling good with drinking, and another 19 percent thought it was fun. Our teens need to know that this is dangerous fun that may cause them heartache and destroy their lives.

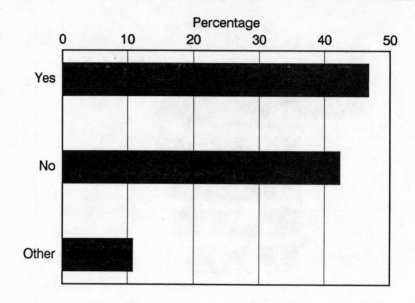

Do you feel booze parties should be raided by the police?

Yes	46.8%
No	42.4%
Sometimes	.9%
No answer	9.9%

Almost half of our teens—and more than that in some schools—feel that booze parties should be raided by the police; yet adults are reluctant to do that. Are teens setting the example for parents—or is it the other way around? Teens see the danger of students who get drunk. Why can't parents, teachers, and law officers work together to put a stop to blatant teen booze parties?

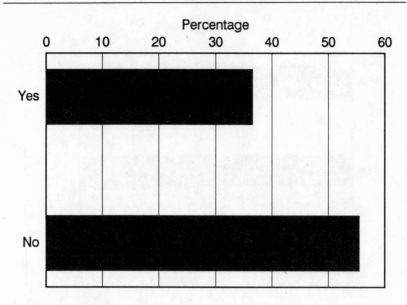

Do you drink alcohol?

Yes	36.6%
No	55.5%
Sometimes	1.1%
No answer	6.8%

Teens seem to have an unusual idea about what it means to drink alcohol. Many of the students who have drunk it answered no to this question but seemed to be regular drinkers. Because they were not drinking at that time, they answered no. Do our teens know what it means to drink? Can they see the danger?

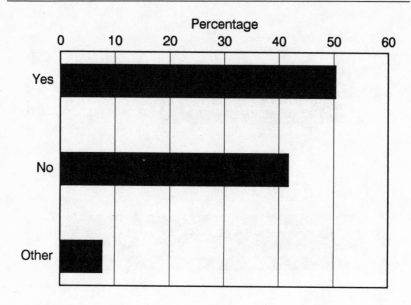

Do either or both of your parents drink alcohol?

Yes	50.4%
No	41.8%
Sometimes	.4%
No answer	7.4%

The statistics concerning those who felt booze parties should be raided by the police and the one for parents who did not use alcohol are very similar. Parents who want their children not to imbibe should keep in mind that teens follow their example. What they see at home may be what they do.

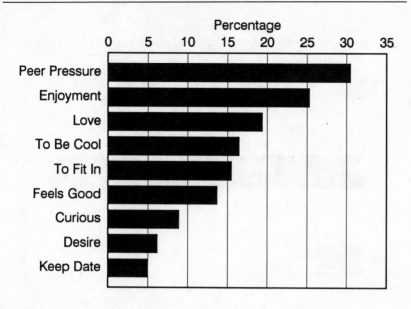

Why do teens have sex?

Peer pressure	30.5%
Pleasure/fun/enjoyment	25.3%
Show love/feel loved	19.4%
To be cool	16.5%
To fit in/acceptance	15.5%
It feels good	13.7%
Curious/experience	8.9%
Urge/desire	6.2%
Keep boyfriend/girlfriend	5.0%

Teens seem to feel they're missing out on something if they don't have sex. The message we've given is that sex is a recreational pastime that makes you feel good. Let's return sex to the commitment of marriage and help teens learn to have sex safely, within the bonds of that commitment.

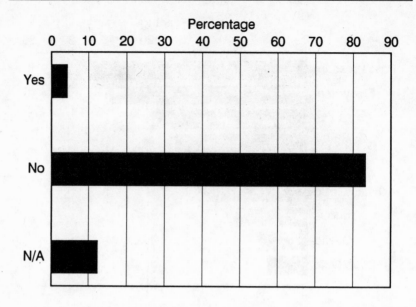

Do you know any teen who has AIDS?

Yes	4.2%
No	83.3%
Did not answer this question	12.5%

Though teens have heard a lot about AIDS, they have only rarely experienced it. Most teens do not know someone with the disease, so it remains distant. To help your teen understand the threat of AIDS, *see* Appendix II.

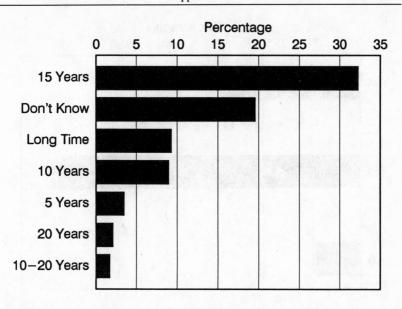

How long do you think AIDS and other sexually transmitted diseases can lie dormant in your body before you know you have them?

15 years	32.3%
I don't know	19.6%
A long time	9.3%
10 years	7.0%
5 years	3.5%
20 years	2.1%
10–20 years	1.7%

Experts disagree on how long the AIDS virus can lie dormant. Some have said fifteen years, while many estimate eight to ten.

Almost a fifth of our teens admitted they didn't know the answer to this question, while another 24.5 didn't answer the question. Even with all the education we've given them, are teens getting the message?

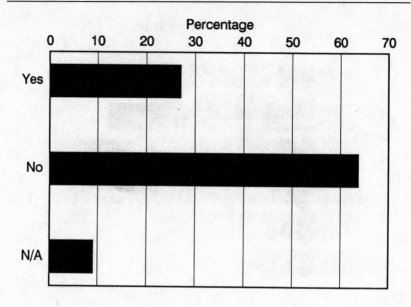

Have you ever had sex?

Yes	27.1%
No	63.8%
No answer	9.1%

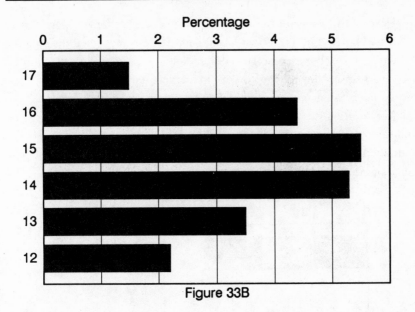

Figure 33B

If yes, at what age did you first experience it?

21	.1%
19	.1%
18	.2%
17	1.5%
16	4.4%
15	5.5%
14	5.3%
13	3.5%
12	2.2%
11	.9%
10	.9%
9	.2%
8	.3%
7	.2%
6	.2%
5	.3%
4	.1%
3	.1%
2	.1%
Did not specify	1.0%

Despite the pressure to have sex, most of our students reported that they had not had it. Teens *can* learn to say no, but they need the support of parents, teachers, and other adults. Note the increase in the numbers who had sex as they reached their mid and late teens. Parents with young teens need to encourage them not to have sex—now!

Notice, too, the sad statistics concerning those who had sex as children—surely cases of abuse! No child is responsible for such a situation. Parents and counselors need to let them know that and encourage them to seek healing.

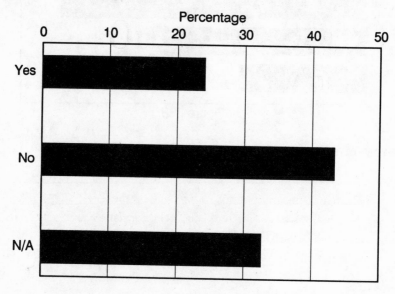

Is it popular to be a virgin in your school?

Yes	24.1%
No	43.3%
No answer	32.6%

Virginity isn't popular, and teens know it! Those who seek popularity all the time will end up with very sad lives. Almost a third of our teens did not answer this question. Perhaps they were embarrassed or thought I had a hidden goal here. It's hard to believe they wouldn't be able to answer this question.

Appendix II
FACTS FOR PARENTS AND TEENS ON DRUGS, ALCOHOL, AND AIDS

I encourage teens and parents to dialogue on these subjects, because some teens will never get a strong message to resist drugs, alcohol, and sex, unless they receive it in the home.

To help parents speak to their teens, I've provided some statistics, facts, and ideas that will show teens that to use drugs or engage in premarital sex is not in their best interest. Give your teens the answers to these questions, because their lives and futures may depend upon it.

Drugs and Alcohol

Why are drugs and alcohol so dangerous? Look at the following chart to see some of the effects alcohol and drug abuse have upon our society. But even that can't begin to count the pain families feel when someone uses drugs, the poor self-esteem they encourage in the drug abuser, and other less tangible results.

Though people may tell you alcohol or drugs will make you relax and feel happy, it isn't entirely true. You may feel good for a short time, but later you will feel worse. For your whole future, you may pay a high price, if you become addicted.

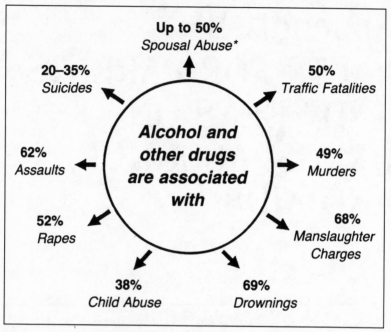

America Has a Big Problem With Alcohol and Other Drugs[1]
As reported in the *National Institute of Alcohol Abuse and Alcoholism Special Report to Congress*, 1983. All other percentages were reported in the *NIAAA Sixth Special Report to Congress*, 1987.

Everyone is using drugs or alcohol, so why shouldn't I? The pressure to use drugs and alcohol *is* high, but *everybody* doesn't use them. Look at some of the statistics on use:

One in 37 high school seniors uses marijuana daily, and 1 in 7 reported using marijuana daily at some time in his or her life (14th and 13th Annual Survey of High School Seniors, respectively, University of Michigan's Institute for Social Research, 1988 data).

One in 23 high school seniors drinks alcohol every day and nearly 2 in 5 become intoxicated at least once every 2 weeks (14th Annual Survey of High School Seniors, University of Michigan's Institute for Social Research, 1988 data).

Thirty-four percent of sixth graders experience peer pressure to use marijuana (*Weekly Reader National Survey of Drugs and Drinking*, spring 1987, Field Publications, Middletown, CT).

Fifty-one percent of sixth graders experience peer pressure to drink beer, wine, or liquor (*Weekly Reader National Survey on Drugs and Drinking*, spring 1987, Field Publications, Middletown, CT).[2]

Consider some of the dangers of alcohol use:

Whereas it can take many years for an adult to become alcoholic, it often takes only 6 to 18 months of heavy drinking for an adolescent to become alcoholic (American Psychiatric Association).[3]

Alcohol-impaired driving is the leading cause of death for young people. In 1986, alcohol-related highway accidents killed nearly 9,000 15- to 24-year-olds, accounting for 38 percent of all alcohol-related highway deaths that year (National Highway Traffic Safety Administration, Fatal Accident Reporting System, 1986).[4]

One-third of all teenagers have problems related to their alcohol consumption (National Institute on Alcohol Abuse and Alcoholism, *Alcohol Consumption and Related Problems*. Alcohol and Health Monograph No. 1, DHHS Pub. No. (ADM) 82-1190, 1982).[5]

About one-fourth of all American homes have been affected by alcohol-related family problems (Gallup Poll, April 1987).[6]

Since alcohol permeates so easily into every cell and organ of the body, it is not surprising that the physical effects of chronic alcohol abuse are wide-ranging and complicated. When large doses of alcohol bathe the body's fluids, the result is metabolic damage in every cell.[7]

Analysis of mortality data on direct or contributing causes of death linked specifically to alcohol showed that death caused by excessive blood alcohol resulted in an average estimated loss of 29.1 years of potential life and death from alcohol abuse resulted in an average estimated loss of 24.1 years of potential life

(National Institute on Alcohol Abuse and Alcoholism, *Sixth Special Report to Congress on Alcohol and Health,* 1987).[8]

Drug or alcohol use *is* a matter of taking your life in your own hands. It can ruin your family, your friendships, and your future. Is it worth any of that?

AIDS

I'm not a homosexual, so I won't get AIDS, will I?   Just because you don't have homosexual sex, you are not safe from getting AIDS. Although AIDS began as a homosexual disease in America, in Africa it is largely a heterosexual disease. How AIDS is transmitted has less to do with the kind of sex you are having than with the fact that you are having sex.

How can you get AIDS?   AIDS is transmitted by blood-to-blood or semen-to-blood contact. That means that you can get AIDS by having heterosexual or homosexual sex or by sharing a needle with someone who's been infected.

But can't I have safe sex if I use a condom?   Condoms cannot provide you with "safe sex," because having sex with someone who has AIDS isn't safe. "Using a condom [during intercourse] . . . only slightly reduces the risk [of getting AIDS] since it can break or leak."[9] Condoms sometimes fail, leaving the uninfected person with no protection at all. It only takes one time for you to become infected. Besides, even so-called safe sex does not help you avoid the emotional suffering of having sex with someone who will not be there in a short time.

I don't know anyone who has AIDS; doesn't that mean I'm safe?
AIDS can take many years to show symptoms—ten years in some cases. If you have sex with someone before he or she knows the disease is in his or her system, you can get it. There is no cure for AIDS. Do you really want to take that risk?

How can I avoid having AIDS?   Avoid having premarital sex. You can't be certain that anyone you have sex with does not have AIDS, if he or she has had sex before. Many people do not have a problem lying to others about their past sexual histories, so even asking is not enough.

The only safe way to avoid AIDS is by abstinence. Then you can be 100 percent sure you do not cause this harm to your body.

You also need to avoid intravenous drug use. Addicts who share needles place themselves at risk.

I'm only a kid. I can't really get AIDS, can I? Whether or not you get AIDS has nothing to do with your age. Look at these statistics:

AIDS "is already the ninth leading cause of death among children 1 to 4 years of age, and the seventh in young people between the ages of 15 and 24. In the latter age group, AIDS deaths have increased 100-fold between 1981 and 1987."

"It is estimated that, by 1991, there will be at least 10,000 to 20,000 HIV-infected children in the United States, and one of every ten pediatric hospital beds will be occupied by a child with AIDS."[10]

AIDS-infected women can pass the disease on to their babies. Teens who have sex or use drugs can get AIDS.

AIDS never improves someone's life. It can only make it worse. But you don't have to have AIDS. The steps are simple. Avoid sex and drugs.

My sex-education teacher says I can have sex, as long as it's safe. Why are you telling me sex isn't safe? Because it isn't. I don't know why your teacher wants to encourage you to have sex, but I do know that AIDS is 100 percent deadly and that condoms fail. You have to make a choice. Do you want the best thing for your life, or do you want to enjoy sex today so much that you'll mortgage your future to a deadly disease?

All of my friends are having sex. How can I be the only one not having it? Because you think enough of yourself not to take part in a dangerous act that will hurt you for a lifetime. Before you consider the two "reasons" to have sex—fun and popularity—consider these good reasons not to have it:

1. *If I don't have sex, I will avoid sexually transmitted diseases.* Avoid sex until you marry and marry a virgin, and you can

avoid AIDS, syphilis, chlamydia, and about fifty other sexually transmitted diseases. AIDS is 100 percent deadly. The results of those STDs can also ruin your life. So why take the chance? It's your life—choose to keep it.

2. *If I don't have sex, I'll never have an illegitimate child.* If you're a girl, you'll never have to choose between an abortion and raising a child without a husband or giving that child up for adoption. If you're a boy, you'll never have to stand by while your girlfriend makes that decision—all the time holding on to the knowledge that this is *your* child.

3. *If I don't have sex, I will never feel emotionally used by an ex-lover.* Even if you don't have sex, you can feel bad when your boyfriend or girlfriend leaves. But at least you haven't given a precious part of your life to that person. It may take time to heal from that loss, but you will not have the memories of your sex life to haunt you forever.

4. *If I don't have sex, I can build stronger relationships.* People may tell you to have sex because it will draw you closer, but in fact, premarital sex short-circuits a strong relationship. Chances are slim that you and your lover will spend time talking about serious topics, giving of yourselves for each other, and learning the basic communication lessons that make a marriage strong. As long as you jump into sex, you will rely on that for your communication needs. But sex outside marriage is selfish and leads nowhere.

5. *If I don't have sex, I'll avoid some bad memories.* Why give yourself the hurt of bad emotions? Why remember the ways you failed by using someone else instead of loving him? Sex outside of marriage does not lead to strong marriages or strong premarital relationships. Why give yourself a memory of failure?

6. *If I don't have sex, I will have a happier sex life in marriage.* When you remember all those premarital relationships, your spouse may not match up with them. By giving yourself all this experience, you pit the person who loves you against previous lovers, who were only there for a short time. Don't mess up your most intimate relationship by filling it with garbage. Save sex

for that important person—the one you want to spend your whole life with.

7. *If I don't have sex, I will please God.* God didn't design sex to be a throwaway relationship. He made it to reinforce the intimacy between a man and wife. When we misuse it, we do not make things better, but worse. We fill up our lives with disease, negative emotions, and guilt.

If you have had sex, God can and will forgive you, but you have to be willing to turn to doing what is right. That means you'll give up sex for the plan He shows us in the Bible. Sex is between two people who are committed to each other in marriage: husband and wife. Anything outside that will only hurt in the long run.

Invest in your own future by turning aside from sex until you are married. If all your friends need to have sex, maybe you need to find some new friends—those who want to invest in their futures, too.

SOURCE NOTES

Chapter 4: How Do I Feel About Myself?

1. *USA Today* (Oct. 18, 1989), 5D.
2. *Psychology Today* (Jan./Feb., 1989), 29–30.
3. *Dallas Morning News* (Oct. 11, 1987), 34A.
4. Josh McDowell, *Research Almanac and Statistical Digest* (Julian, Calif.: Julian Press, 1990), 104.

Chapter 5: What Are My Problems?

1. *USA Today* (Oct. 2, 1989), 1D.
2. *USA Today* (Sept. 13, 1989), 1D.
3. Josh McDowell, *Research Almanac and Statistical Digest* (Julian, Calif.: Julian Press, 1990), 126.
4. *USA Today* (Sept. 27, 1989), 24.
5. McDowell, *Almanac*, 148.
6. Dennis Kelly, "Drug Fears Fall When Kids Feel Immortal," *USA Today* (Feb. 26, 1990), 1A.

7. Valerie Lynn Dorsey, "Alcohol Abuse Tops Coaches' Concerns," *USA Today* (Jan. 31, 1990), 12C.
8. McDowell, *Almanac*, 1.
9. "Cheating, Sex and Kids' Scruples," *USA Today* (Feb. 1, 1990), 1D.
10. "Top Threat to Family Is No Time for Kids," *Chicago Tribune* (Oct. 10, 1989), 9.
11. *Signs of the Times* (Dec., 1989), 6.

Chapter 6: Whom Do I Look Up To?

1. *USA Today* (Nov. 30, 1989).
2. Josh McDowell, *Research Almanac and Statistical Digest* (Julian, Calif.: Julian Press, 1990), 88.
3. Ibid., 89.

Chapter 7: What Am I Learning From My Parents?

1. Josh McDowell, *Research Almanac and Statistical Digest* (Julian, Calif.: Julian Press, 1990), 101.
2. Ibid.
3. Ibid., 102.
4. Ibid., 103.
5. Ibid., 102.

Chapter 8: How Would I Solve America's Problems?

1. William J. Bennett and C. Everett Koop, "Statement on AIDS Education," a letter published by the U.S. Department of Education (Jan. 30, 1987).

Chapter 9: Why Do I Sometimes Make Poor Decisions?

1. "Nation," *The Boston Globe* (Jan. 10, 1990).
2. *US News & World Report* (Aug. 14, 1989), 70.
3. Ibid.
4. Ibid.
5. Josh McDowell, *Research Almanac and Statistical Digest* (Julian, Calif.: Julian Press, 1990), 2–3.
6. Louis Harris and Associates, Inc., "American Teens Speak: Sex, Myth, TV and Birth Control," *The Planned Parenthood Poll* (Sept./Oct., 1986), 21.

7. McDowell, *Almanac*, 13.
8. "Sharp Rise in Sex-Related Diseases," *New York Times Health* (July 14, 1988), 234.
9. *US News & World Report* (June 2, 1986), 53.
10. Joe S. McIlthany, M.D., *CMS Journal*, 18, no. 1 (Winter, 1987), 27–30.

Chapter 10: What's Going on in School?

1. *AFA Journal* (Sept., 1989), 24.
2. Josh McDowell, *Research Almanac and Statistical Digest* (Julian, Calif.: Julian Press, 1990), 104.
3. *Life* (July, 1989), 30.
4. *USA Today* (May 15, 1986), 5D.
5. McDowell, *Almanac*, 12.

Chapter 11: What Do We Expect of Our Schools?

1. National Commission on Excellence in Education, "A Nation at Risk," *The Great School Debate*, Beatrice and Ronald Gross, eds. (New York: Touchstone/Simon & Schuster, 1985), 32.
2. Karen De Witt, "Verbal Scores Hit New Low in Scholastic Aptitude Tests," *New York Times* (Aug. 27, 1991), A1.
3. National Commission, "A Nation," 33.
4. Kathryn D. Sloane, "Home Influences on Talent Development," *Developing Talent in Young People*, ed. Benjamin S. Bloom (New York: Ballantine Books, 1985), 440–442.

Chapter 12: A Psychology of Education

1. Ed. Phyllis Schlafly, *Child Abuse in the Classroom* (Westchester, Ill.: Crossway Books, 1985), 14.
2. State of Michigan in the Circuit Court of Saint Joseph, deposition of William R. Coulson, Ph.D., *Network Reporting* (Feb. 21–22, 1991), 119.
3. Raymond H. Corsini, *Roleplaying in Psychotherapy* (Chicago: Aldine Pub. Co., 1966), 10–11.
4. Ibid., 199.
5. "Q.R. [Quieting Reflex] Guided Imagery and Meditation," ProFamily Forum.

6. Rachel Copelan, *How to Hypnotize Yourself and Others* (New York: Harper & Row, Pubs., 1982), 20.
7. "Success Unlimited," *Heritage News Paper News Herald* (May 16, 1990), 5-B.
8. Copelan, *How to Hypnotize*, 3.
9. Michigan Model for Comprehensive School Health Education, Grade 7, Module 2, Lesson 7, 261.
10. Ibid., xiv, emphasis added.
11. Ibid.
12. Copelan, *How to Hypnotize*, 9–10.
13. Schlafly, *Child Abuse.*
14. W.R. Coulson, Ph.D., "Founder of 'Value Free' Education Says He Owes Parents an Apology," *American Family Association Journal* (April, 1989), 20, 21.

Chapter 13: The Flaws in Affective Education

1. State of Michigan in the Circuit Court of Saint Joseph, deposition of William R. Coulson, Ph.D., *Network Reporting* (Feb. 21–22, 1991).
2. Thomas E. Elkins, M.D., "On the Need for More Careful Consideration of Sex Education Programs in the Schools," 5.
3. P.A. 185 of 1987, State of Michigan, 84th Legislature, Regular Session of 1987, Sec. 1169.
4. *Michigan HIV/AIDS Report*, 6, no. 3 (March 1991), 5.
5. A letter from Janet Bierlein to Bob Lemieux at the DADS Foundation (Dec. 5, 1989).
6. Elkins, "On the Need," 6.
7. Ibid., 8.

Chapter 14: Challenging Parenthood

1. Michigan Model for Comprehensive School Health Education, Grade 5, 217.
2. Human Development/Sex Education Program, Gobles Public Schools, Gobles, Michigan.
3. Ibid., 17.

Appendix II: Facts for Parents and Teens

1. *Prevention Plus II* (Rockville, Md.: National Clearinghouse for Alcohol and Drug Information, n.d.), 3.
2. Ibid., 6.
3. Ibid., 6.
4. Ibid., 7.
5. Ibid.
6. Ibid.
7. *The Columbia University College of Physicians & Surgeons Complete Home Medical Guide* (New York: Crown Pubs., 1989), 365.
8. *Prevention Plus II*, 7.
9. *Columbia University Guide*, 487.
10. "The Ominous Threat of Pediatric AIDS," *AIDS Protection* (Feb., 1990), 3.

SUGGESTED READING

SUGGESTED READING

Books for Teens

Bertolini, Dewey. *Sometimes I Really Hate You.* Wheaton, Ill.: Victor Books, 1991. Outlines five steps to winning the battle over bitterness in your life.

Peterson, Lorraine. *Anybody Can Be Cool, But Awesome Takes Practice.* Minneapolis, Minn.: Bethany House Pubs., 1988. A teen devotional that challenges and inspires young people to let God's truth shape their self-images.

Peterson, Lorraine. *If God Loves Me, Why Can't I Get My Locker Open.* Minneapolis, Minn.: Bethany House Pubs., 1983. Teen daily devotional with snapshot stories from youngsters' worlds, which provide biblical conclusions.

Robbins, Duffy. *It's How You Play the Game.* Wheaton, Ill.: Victor Books, 1991. Short, funny stories for everyday life and practical lessons from the life of David, in the Bible. Running through them all is the story of God, who coaches His children through victories and defeats.

Sanders, Bill. *Goalposts: Devotions for Girls*. Old Tappan, N. J.: Fleming H. Revell Co., 1990. Practical devotions for girls, which provide help with self-esteem and avoiding negative peer pressure, and show them how to live a strong Christian life.

Sanders, Bill. *Goalposts: Devotions for Guys*. Old Tappan, N. J.: Fleming H. Revell Co., 1990. Practical devotions for guys, which provide help with self-esteem and avoiding negative peer pressure, and show them how to live a strong Christian life.

Sanders, Bill. *Life, Sex, and Everything in Between*. Tarrytown, N. Y.: Fleming H. Revell Co., 1991. Answers to the questions teens ask about themselves, their relationships with others, and their homes.

Sanders, Bill. *Outtakes: Devotions for Girls*. Old Tappan, N. J.: Fleming H. Revell Co., 1988. Devotions that help girls face up to peer pressure and deal with topics such as drugs, suicide, and family life.

Sanders, Bill. *Outtakes, Devotions for Guys*. Old Tappan, N. J.: Fleming H. Revell Co., 1988. Devotions that help guys face up to peer pressure and deal with topics such as drugs, suicide, and family life.

St. Clair, Barry. *The Big Man on Campus*. Wheaton, Ill.: Victor Books, 1991. Jesus Christ is the Big Man on Campus. You can get to know Him in this book, and you'll never be the same.

Soaries, Buster. *My Family Is Driving Me Crazy*. Wheaton, Ill.: Victor Books, 1991. Describes how to move from survival to satisfaction at home by learning practical ways to open up communication and increase understanding.

Books for Parents

Child Abuse

Morrison, Jan. *A Safe Place (Beyond Sexual Abuse)*. Wheaton, Ill.: Harold Shaw Pubs., 1990. This book was written to encourage victims of sexual abuse to uncover the lies it creates and grow to understand the truth about love and sexuality.

Ross, Ron. *When I Grow Up I Want to Be an Adult*. San Diego, Calif.: Recovery Publications, 1990. Ron Ross's personal story is told of tragedy and triumph over childhood abuse. It offers a way to achieve similar successes and a workbook that introduces the value of the twelve-step recovery process to Christians raised in dysfunctional families.

Vredevelt, Pamela and Kathryn Rodriguez, *Surviving the Secret*. Old Tappan, N. J.: Fleming H. Revell Co., 1987. Help for adults who want to identify and heal the hurts of sexual child abuse.

Christian Living Aids

Abraham, Ken. *The Disillusioned Christian (Advice for the Burned and Burned Out)*. San Bernadino, Calif.: Here's Life Publishers, 1991. Real-life, hopeful answers for the burned and burned-out believer.

Campolo, Tony. *You Can Make the Difference*. Waco, Tex.: Word Books, 1984. A biblical outlook on commitment, vocation, dating, and discipleship.

Carnegie, Dale. *How to Win Friends and Influence People*. New York: Simon & Schuster, 1964. A practical and useful handbook on facing the problems of getting along with and influencing people in your everyday business and social contacts. Though not specifically Christian, it provides many helpful guidelines.

Hemfelt, Dr. Robert, Dr. Frank Minirth, Dr. Paul Meier. *We Are Driven.* Nashville, Tenn.: Thomas Nelson Publishers, 1991. The doctors suggest ten touchstones for living a balanced life within our culture that chases the false gods of materialism and achievement.

Hybels, Bill. *Honest to God (Becoming an Authentic Christian).* Grand Rapids, Mich.: Zondervan Publishing House, 1990. A challenge to Christians to examine their life-styles, go beyond just talking about faith, and be permeated with Christianity.

Hybels, Bill. *Too Busy to Pray.* Downers Grove, Il.: InterVarsity Press, 1988. Life principals for every Christian who is serious about taking his relationship with God from his head to his heart.

Hybels, Bill. *Who You Are When No One Is Looking.* Downers Grove, Ill.: InterVarsity Press, 1987. A biblical look at choosing consistency and resisting compromise in your Christian walk.

Littauer, Florence. *Dare to Dream.* Dallas, Tex.: Word Publishing, 1991. Dreams add imagination to our goals, visions to our plans, and hope to our futures. Florence applies her well-known system of personality analysis to the subject of making dreams come true.

McGee, Robert S. *Search for Significance.* Houston, Tex.: Rapha Publishers, 1990. Building your self-worth on the love and forgiveness of Jesus Christ and not on worldly standards.

Swindoll, Chuck. *Living Above the Level of Mediocrity.* Waco, Tex.: Word Books, 1987. Challenges readers to confront mediocrity through personal commitment, refocusing priorities, and conquering stagnation and selfishness.

Communication

Wright, H. Norman. *How to Speak Your Spouse's Language*. Old Tappan, N. J.: Fleming H. Revell Co., 1986. A valuable guide to improving communication with your spouse. The same principles can be used to improve your communication with others, too.

Youth for Christ. *How to Get Your Teenager to Talk to You*. Wheaton, Ill.: Victor Books, 1988. Chuck Swindoll, Jay Kesler, Josh McDowell, Ron Hutchcraft, Howard Hendricks, Anthony Campolo, and many more well-known authors review rules of good adult communication that apply to communication between adults and teenagers.

Parenting

Anthony, T. Mitchel. *Suicide—Knowing When Your Teen Is at Risk*. Ventura, Calif.: Regal Books, 1991. A look at suicide prevention that helps parents see teenage pain and set practical, workable answers in motion.

Aranza, Jacob. *Lord! Why Is My Child a Rebel? (Parents and Kids in Crisis)*. Lafayette, La.: Huntington House, 1990. A biblical look at kids in rebellion, with many tips for parents.

Campbell, Ross, et al. *How to Raise Christian Kids in a Non-Christian World*. Wheaton, Ill.: Victor Books, 1988. Realistic advice on teaching young people how to distinguish between right and wrong, without getting into the legalism trap.

Collins, Gary, et al. *Parents and Children*. Wheaton, Ill.: Youth for Christ, 1986. A guide to solving problems and building relationships in marriage and parenting.

A dad named Bill. *Daddy, I'm Pregnant*. Portland, Ore.: Multnomah Press, 1987. A collection of a father's journal entries during the nine months of his daughter's pregnancy. A real help for parents with a similar situation.

Hansel, Tim. *What Kids Need Most in a Dad*. Old Tappan, N. J.: Fleming H. Revell Co., 1989. A realistic guide for fathers, to help them become skillful parents. Includes specific tips and activities.

Kesler, Dr. Jay. *Family Forum*. Wheaton, Ill.: Victor Books, 1984. Dr. Kesler answers your questions about family relationships and other critical issues. He speaks from the foundations of biblical truth and personal experience.

Kesler, Jay. *Parents and Teenagers*. Wheaton, Ill.: Victor Books, 1984. A practical guide to solving problems and building relationships.

Kesler, Jay, *Ten Mistakes Parents Make With Teenagers (and How to Avoid Them)*. Brentwood, Tenn.: Wolgemuth & Hyatt Pubs., 1988. Covers the top ten mistakes parents make with their teenagers. Parents will be able to identify their own mistakes and find out what to do about them.

Laurent, Dr. Robert. *Keeping Your Teen in Touch with God*. Elgin, Ill.: David C. Cook Pub. Co., 1988. Practical help for parents and youth workers in dealing with issues that alienate teens from the church and weaken their relationships with God.

Leman, Dr. Kevin. *Making Your Children Mind Without*

Losing Yours. Old Tappan, N. J.: Fleming H. Revell Co., 1987. Using reality discipline, learn to make your children mind lovingly, wisely, and well.

McDowell, Josh. *What I Wish My Parents Knew About My Sexuality.* San Bernadino, Calif.: Here's Life Publishers, 1987. Through data from surveys, interviews, response sheets and essays, discusses what's going on in a teen's world. Also shows realistically why the young people should wait for sex and gives practical guidelines to help them with self-control.

Murray, Stephen and Randy Smith. *Divorce Recovery for Teenagers.* Grand Rapids, Mich.: Zondervan Publishing House, 1990. How to help your kids recover, heal, and grow when your family is ripped apart.

Sanders, Bill. *Almost Everything Teens Want Parents to Know.* Old Tappan, N. J.: Fleming H. Revell Co., 1987. Nineteen messages teens have shared concerning how their parents can meet their needs, and practical advice on how parents can do that.

Smalley, Gary. *The Key to Your Child's Heart.* Dallas, Tex.: Word Publishing, 1984. Outlines several basic principals that are key to raising children and maintaining a close-knit family.